"*Distinctly You* is an important book for today's woman. With personal vulnerability on her own journey, Cheryl gives a distinct road map to internal freedom, wholeness, and growth. I highly recommend women's groups use this for their study together."

—Leslie Vernick, licensed counselor, relationship coach, speaker, and author of seven books, including the bestselling *The Emotionally Destructive Marriage*

distinctly you

Trading Comparison and Competition for Freedom and Fulfillment

cheryl martin

BETHANYHOUSE
a division of Baker Publishing Group
Minneapolis, Minnesota

© 2016 by Cheryl Martin

Published by Bethany House Publishers
11400 Hampshire Avenue South
Bloomington, Minnesota 55438
www.bethanyhouse.com

Bethany House Publishers is a division of
Baker Publishing Group, Grand Rapids, Michigan

Printed in the United States of America

Library of Congress Cataloging-in-Publication Data is on file at the Library of Congress, Washington, DC.

Library of Congress Control Number: 2015956689

ISBN: 978-0-7642-1586-5

Scripture quotations, unless otherwise noted, are from the Holy Bible, New International Version®. NIV®. Copyright © 1973, 1978, 1984, 2011 by Biblica, Inc.™ Used by permission of Zondervan. All rights reserved worldwide. www.zondervan.com

Scripture quotations marked THE MESSAGE are from The Message by Eugene H. Peterson, copyright © 1993, 1994, 1995, 2000, 2001, 2002. Used by permission of NavPress Publishing Group. All rights reserved.

Scripture quotations marked NLT are from the Holy Bible, New Living Translation, copyright © 1996, 2004, 2007 by Tyndale House Foundation. Used by permission of Tyndale House Publishers, Inc., Carol Stream, Illinois 60188. All rights reserved.

Scripture quotations marked NKJV are from the New King James Version. Copyright © 1982 by Thomas Nelson, Inc. Used by permission. All rights reserved.

Scripture quotations marked KJV are from the King James Version of the Bible.

Cover design by Brand Navigation

Author is represented by Books & Such Literary Agency.

16 17 18 19 20 21 22   7 6 5 4 3 2 1

To my beloved mother, Ormie Martin,
one distinct woman

Contents

Part Two: Distinctly You Builders

Introduction

Have you ever heard anyone say, "My ultimate dream is to be *average*"? I haven't. I don't know anyone who's born with a desire to be mediocre or to accomplish nothing in life. If you're like me, you want to stand out, be special, the best you can be, distinctive.

Well, that is also God's desire for you. He does nothing haphazard, without purpose. It's all meticulously planned. He determined our looks, personality, heritage, intelligence, and gender. So that means there is something specific He wants you to accomplish as *you*, with your specific blend of abilities. It may take a while to know what it is, to develop into that *you*, and to be totally comfortable with your uniqueness.

I'm quite familiar with the journey. I'm still on it. The struggle to accept my distinctiveness began early for me. Maybe it's because I have seven brothers and no sisters. My mother said she went to the hospital each time hoping for a girl. On the seventh try her prayer was answered. I was born.

Being the only girl among so many boys made me special from day one. But in just a few short years, without any coaching, I started secretly comparing my looks and complexion with brother #6 (Darrell), my girl cousins, classmates, and church girls.

I noticed that I looked nothing like Darrell. He was extremely fair. I was very dark. He was adorable. I was very average looking. One day my mother told me a story that confirmed my insecurity. She said when I was born there was a steady stream of traffic to our house. Visitors would come, look at me, whisper to each other, and then leave without saying much.

At first she thought it was because the Martins finally had a girl. Then she found out it was about much more. Because I looked nothing like four-year-old Darrell, the one closest to me in age, and I was considerably darker than most of my brothers—and my parents—some visitors were questioning my paternity. My mother said one person asked, "What is Rev. Martin saying?" She answered, "When he gets worried, I'll let you know." Of course, my father wasn't saying anything because he knew I was his daughter. Plus, he thought I resembled his deceased mother.

There is something specific He wants you to accomplish as you, with your specific blend of abilities.

At times I wondered, "Why did God make me look so different from my mother?" I thought she was pretty and my father handsome. When I looked at myself, I could not see my mother in me. This hurt. I told no one about this ongoing dialogue, except God. I struggled year after year with this inward battle.

I compared myself with my friends in grade school. I knew which ones were favored because they were pretty. I knew which ones got invited to the popular birthday parties because they were cute. I admired the church girls who got asked out because they were *fine*. I was never in these exclusive groups.

When your focus is always on what's "wrong" with you, you diminish what's "right" about you. That's what I did for years. Even though I was soaring academically, my focus was on my shortcomings.

No matter how put together we may look on the outside, we all face challenges and roadblocks to being the person we desperately want to be, the person God created us to be. All my life I've been pressing through the barriers, purposing to never lose hope. I've discovered that God will help us when this is our determined focus.

In order to thrive in your uniqueness and be distinct, you need to be aware of what I call "Distinctly You Blockers" and then overpower them with "Distinctly You Builders." I don't claim to know everything about them, but I believe that what I've learned so far can help you stay in the race (or get back in it), get revved up, and win it. These are proven principles I've applied in my own life.

On this journey to becoming distinctly you, it's important to remember that we can only realize this goal if our definition of *distinct* is what God had in mind. Why? He created us. We are His idea. You were in His mind before you were conceived. David says in Psalm 139:13–16 (NLT):

> You . . . knit me together in my mother's womb. Thank you for making me so wonderfully complex! Your workmanship is marvelous. . . . You saw me before I was born. Every day of

my life was recorded in your book. Every moment was laid out
before a single day had passed.

Because only God holds the rights to our distinctive life story,
He alone knows the most direct path to get us there. I love how
Psalm 32:8 puts it in the *New Living Translation*: "The Lord
says, 'I will guide you along the *best* pathway for your life'"
(emphasis mine).

I've added questions at the end of each chapter to assist you
in becoming distinctly you. I encourage you to respond immediately after reading each chapter and reflect on your takeaways.
It's a great way to internalize the principles and then pledge
to make the necessary changes to thrive. You may want to join
with a few others to read and discuss the book together. Use
the questions to prompt your discussion.

What would happen if you approached every God-given assignment, every opportunity, with the mindset that there are
no barriers, no limitations, and nothing holding you back? If
you are a Christ follower, obedient to the call on your life, there
are no impediments that you cannot victoriously overcome in
your quest. As David says, "The battle is the Lord's" (1 Samuel
17:47). Walk in that truth. Let *Distinctly You* guide you along
your journey. Let's get started.

Part One

Distinctly You
Blockers

1

Letting Others Define You

My most devastating experience in high school was taking Advanced Placement (AP) English my senior year. English was one of my best subjects. I had made only A's (except for one B), so I was confident I would do well in this class, even though I was attending what was considered the best public high school in Houston.

I grew up in the predominantly black Fifth Ward neighborhood, located a few minutes from downtown Houston. After graduating from a neighborhood junior high school, where I was the class valedictorian, I elected to take part in a voluntary desegregation program, in which I could transfer to any school where I would be in the minority, and get free transportation. I chose Bellaire High School.

Back then, I wanted to be distinct. I believed that an education at a top high school would stretch me as well as provide great college preparatory classes. I was right about both, but what I did not count on was that this experience would also rock my confidence. I was used to being an achiever where everyone looked like me. I was comfortable. But I had never in my life been thrust into a situation where I was in the minority.

Even though I had been an honor student all my life, when I enrolled at Bellaire in the tenth grade, the administrator did not place me in advanced classes. Neither my mother nor I questioned it. But when I realized that Bellaire had accelerated classes, I signed myself up for those the following year. I couldn't help but think, *Did the school administrator neglect to enroll me in those classes because I was black and he didn't think I could handle them?*

I did well my first and second years at Bellaire but ran into a major problem my senior year in AP English. There were three black students in the class. My teacher loved the two black guys, and I admired them as well. They were extremely bright and had been in AP classes from the beginning. (They went on to attend Harvard and Princeton.) I was quiet and somewhat withdrawn in the class. One day, the teacher told me I could not write, and she was giving me a C in the class. She said that if I wanted to stay in AP English, I would need to bring my grades up.

I was absolutely devastated. *I can't write? I can't write?!* I rehearsed her words over and over again. It didn't matter that I had never been told this before. It didn't matter that I had aced most of my English classes. Here was this teacher telling me I was a failure (which is how I saw it), and my self-esteem hit rock bottom.

We are taught to believe what our parents, teachers, and other adults tell us. They are the experts. On the other hand, I couldn't believe I had made it this far, was applying to college, and was now getting this negative report at this pivotal time in my life.

I lost almost all confidence. Proverbs 18:21 says, "The tongue has the power of life and death." This teacher spoke "death" to my soul. Here I was this confident girl (academically), and now I was afraid to apply to the college of my dreams because of what my teacher said. I was emotionally paralyzed. I wasn't sure what I was doing wrong. I also believed she just didn't like me. She never did. We had no rapport, no chemistry. Nonetheless, I worked hard to bring up my grades.

For this painful season in my life, I allowed this teacher's opinion of me to define me. Her tone was one of authority and confidence when she handed down her verdict about me. I failed to remember my previous track record in English. I took the word of this one teacher. I meditated on those words—that I could not write. I refused to let them go. They became a part of me, lodged in my brain, and affected my psyche for years.

Has someone told you, "You aren't pretty enough." "You aren't smart enough." "You're too fat!" "You can't get a boyfriend!" "That's the best you can do." "You're too old to do that." "You're wasting your time"? These indictments are like a fast-moving cancer. Once they get inside you, they will sap your dreams and steal your vitality for living. You have given someone else the power to define you, a power that belongs only to God. That's what I did. My demeanor changed overnight. I felt like such a failure. I was overcome with fear when I was asked to write something, anything. That's the power of a negative word or opinion.

My perception of myself changed completely, all because of one indictment. Maybe I wasn't as smart as I'd thought. I wanted to go to one of the top colleges, Northwestern University, but I began thinking that maybe I needed to scrap that dream because my teacher said I was not a good writer.

Whenever you let others define you and your essence, you block your progress to thriving in your own uniqueness. You prevent yourself from becoming the distinct person God called you to be. I came very close to discarding my dreams because of that teacher's view of me, until God stepped in with His emissary to encourage me to pursue the dreams He had placed in my heart.

Whenever you let others define you and your essence, you block your progress to thriving in your own uniqueness.

One afternoon during my junior year of high school, my mother suggested I call the commercial FM Christian radio station in Houston, KFMK, to inquire about a part-time job. I told the person who answered the phone that I was interested in a career in broadcasting and wondered if the station had any internships or jobs for students. The gentleman said, "No, not unless we think you're talented." I paused, and then he said, "Well, are you going to come in?" Of course, I said yes. I had no idea that I was talking to the station manager, Burt Perrault. I had an interview with him, and he hired me. He became my first mentor. After a few lessons on operating the audio board, I worked my first Saturday four-hour on-air shift. I was so excited. In addition to playing music, I read the news at the top of the hour. This weekend job confirmed my interest in a broadcasting career.

One day Mr. Perrault told me I should apply to Northwestern University in Evanston, Illinois, because it had one of the best programs in speech and journalism. I had not heard of Northwestern until my junior year, when I discovered that two championship debaters from my high school were planning to attend. I thought it must be an excellent school because these guys were going. After Mr. Perrault mentioned it, I looked up information about the university, and it seemed like a perfect match for what I desired in a college experience. I had prayed specifically, telling the Lord I wanted to go to a medium-sized, co-ed, private university near the big city, but not in it, with an excellent academic program in broadcasting.

My mother and I attended a local presentation by Northwestern for prospective students. We were impressed with what we heard, but my mother acknowledged that the school was way out of our price range. Practically every college was out of our price range, for that matter. My father was a barber in our neighborhood. My mother had a beauty shop in the back of the house. She did say, though, that we should pray about it because there was nothing too hard for God.

During this time, it seemed as if almost every day Mr. Perrault asked me if I had applied to Northwestern. I didn't dare tell him what my teacher had said. I finally told my mother I would go ahead and apply so Mr. Perrault would stop asking me. I wanted to appease him. I thought I had a chance to get in, since I was in the top percent of my class of 738 students. I applied without saying a word to my English teacher.

In hindsight, God used Mr. Perrault to encourage me while another adult had discouraged me. He saw me as an achiever, someone with natural talent. My English teacher saw me as a mediocre student. No matter how hard I worked in class, she never saw me differently.

I decided not to take the AP English test for college credit based on her opinion of me. I did take the pre-exam in class, and I remember scoring higher on the test than many of my peers. My teacher never said a word about my results.

I was shocked and elated when Northwestern admitted me. I should not have been, since I had good grades. I received an outstanding financial aid package that required my parents to contribute an amount they could afford. I knew this was God working on my behalf, but I still had no intention of sharing the good news with my English teacher.

One day she found out through the grapevine that I had been admitted to Northwestern. There were no congratulations. Instead of being happy for me, she said very sternly, "You're going to have to work really hard, especially on your writing, if you're going to make it." One more dagger thrust into my heart. I took her words with me, trembling, to NU. Those words choked me for years, stifling me. No matter what I accomplished, I heard them. I allowed her words to define me.

becoming distinctly you

1. Who have you allowed to define you negatively and why?
2. What has been the impact on your life (choices, personality, emotions)?
3. Proverbs 18:21 says, "The tongue has the power of life and death." What "death" words and opinions have defined you negatively that you need to release?
4. Who has God used to speak words of "life" to you? What difference has it made?

2

Letting *You* Define You

I arrived on my college campus as a freshman, excited, yet pensive. I did take my English teacher's warning seriously and registered for a writing class each quarter. I also had access to a tutor. I worked hard in these courses and made A's. The grades, however, could not undo the mark *inadequate* stamped on me by my teacher.

I enrolled in the school of speech, majoring in radio-TV-film. I thought I had an edge over my fellow students because I had worked at the local radio station in Houston for more than a year before college. In addition to my Saturday radio shift, I also held other jobs at the station, plus I had an internship that exposed me to the various management positions available in radio and television. I thought that was pretty impressive for a teenager. Well, I overlooked the fact that Northwestern University attracted only the top students from all over the country, nothing but achievers. It didn't take long to realize in my introductory radio-television class that while I was good, I was not the best among my peers. Some had more experience. Others were smarter. That smug feeling left me quickly. I was disheartened. I wanted to quit. If I couldn't be distinct, why play at all?

After my freshman year, I decided to transfer to the liberal arts school on campus and major in history. Maybe I would set my sights on a career as a lawyer. I was there for only one quarter. What happened? God in His providence allowed me to have a long conversation one evening with a campus administrator. I had a work-study job in his office. He asked how things were going. I told him about my decision to switch from the school of speech to the liberal arts school.

I poured out my heart to him about feeling inadequate and disappointed that I was not a star student. What I remember most about that fateful evening is that he encouraged me to "go back and get in the race." I'm so glad he did. Because of his pep talk, I immediately filled out the paper work to return to the school of speech the next quarter. I believe our conversation was divine intervention to get me back on my God-ordained path.

Just because you are not the best does not mean you don't have a right to be there or that you can't be a success. It is so easy to tell God no based on what we are not. This happens when we look inward instead of outward and focus on circumstances that are less than ideal. If we look at ourselves and what's wrong with us long enough, depression can set in, and a defeatist attitude can take over.

Gideon is a great example of this. An angel of the Lord appeared to him during dire circumstances and said, "The Lord is with you, mighty warrior" (Judges 6:12). The angel called Gideon a mighty warrior. But Gideon called himself the least in the weakest family (v. 15). How long had Gideon defined himself this way? How often did he remind himself that in the weakest family, he was the least? How destructive was this self-talk? It was so destructive that after the angel of the Lord told him what God's assignment was for him, he was in shock. "Pardon me, my lord," Gideon replied, "but how can I save Israel?" (Judges 6:15). The angel repeated what he told Gideon earlier: You can do this for one reason. God will be with you (v. 16).

Just because you are not the best does not mean that you can't be a success.

God on our side is the game-changer. It doesn't matter how the odds are stacked against us, where we grew up, what we look like, or what our inadequacies are. When God shows up and gives us our assignment, He promises to go with us. The angel told Gideon, "Go in the strength you have. . . . Am I not sending you?" (Judges 6:14). God has access to our résumés. He knows all of our accomplishments. He is not impressed. He knows all of our inadequacies. He is not discouraged. His strength is made perfect in our weaknesses (see 2 Corinthians 12:9).

Gideon could have been Moses' distant cousin. They both suffered from negative self-talk. When God called out to Moses from an unlikely place (a burning bush) and told him who He was and then gave Moses his assignment ("I am sending you to Pharaoh to bring my people the Israelites out of Egypt" [Exodus 3:10]), Moses immediately went inward with self-focus. Here was the God of the universe talking, the God who speaks and it is done, the God who created him, setting his agenda, and all Moses could think about was himself and his own sense of inadequacy. "But Moses said to God, 'Who am I, that I should go to Pharaoh and

23

bring the Israelites out of Egypt?'" (Exodus 3:11). God probably wanted to shout at that point and say, "Moses, it's not about *you*! It's about *me* and *my power*! You're just the conduit." Instead, God answered, "I will be with you" (Exodus 3:12). In other words, "All you need to succeed when I've called you to a task is to remember that I am with you. It doesn't mean that it will be easy, without struggles and battles, but I will be with you every step of the way." We should be wherever God wants us to be at the time. Success is not promised to the best and the brightest. Success from God's perspective is guaranteed to those who are seeking His guidance and following the path He ordained.

I graduated from Northwestern with a strong GPA and was elected to two honorary societies. A couple of years later, I returned to pursue a master's degree in broadcast journalism. NBC News hired me right out of graduate school (more about that later).

As a freshman, I was using the wrong measuring sticks (my peers' strengths and *my* expectations) to determine my worth and to define *distinction*. God never uses someone else's talents and abilities as the plumb line for our achievement. It's a great distraction of Satan to get us focused on what everyone else in the room has, what we *don't* have (as I was doing in my freshman class), and what we think we need. If we look long enough, we'll get discouraged, slow down, and possibly drop out of the race of life altogether.

The great thing about this journey is that He is *Emmanuel*—God with us. While I was stuck, God wasn't. He did not leave me. I felt His presence daily as He quietly and lovingly began to uncover what was holding me back from being *distinct*. Be careful of letting *you* define you to a lesser role than you were created to play.

becoming distinctly
you

1. Name a time you walked away from an opportunity because of a sense of inadequacy.

2. What have you dreamed of doing but haven't because of an inaccurate view of yourself?

3. Gideon called himself the "least in the weakest family." How do you describe yourself?

4. What measuring sticks are you using to determine your self-worth?

5. Are you relegating yourself to a lesser role than God called you to play? If so, why?

3

Those Three C's: Comparing, Competing, Coveting

Satan loves to distract us with the triplets: comparing, competing, and coveting. Those three C's can lead to three D's: depression, discouragement, and discontentment. They can also be deadly. Remember the tragic story of the first sons, Cain and Abel, in Genesis 4? When they grew up, Cain became a farmer. Abel was a shepherd. When the time came to present a gift to the Lord, Cain presented some of his crops and Abel brought the best of his firstborn lambs. The Lord accepted Abel's gift but not Cain's. Why? Not because He preferred lamb over grain, but because Abel gave God his *best*. Cain became very angry. The Lord asked Cain, "Why are you angry?" (v. 6). Then He told him in verse 7, "If you do what is right, will you not be accepted?" What's the right thing? It is to do our best in every instance. That is what makes us distinctive. Galatians

6:4 (NLT) puts it this way: "Pay careful attention to your own work, for then you will get the satisfaction of a job well done, and you won't need to compare yourself to anyone else."

Comparison, competition, and covetousness ate at Cain until he murdered his own brother. God had warned him in advance: "But if you do not do what is right, sin is crouching at your door; it desires to have you, but you must rule over it" (Genesis 4:7).

Those three C's can lead to three D's: depression, discouragement, and discontentment.

Have you ever murdered another woman with your words, simply because she did *her* best, you did not, and she was rewarded big time? You were not genuinely happy about her success. You may have secretly resented it. It's dangerous when we constantly compare ourselves to others. One of two things will happen: Either pride and arrogance or depression and inferiority will set in.

It is easy to get caught in this trap of measuring our success by someone else. I've been guilty of this. It is so unhealthy, and it keeps us from living the victorious life. The struggle can eat up our insides. I remember when I was in between television jobs. I spent a lot of time watching other anchors deliver the news. I noticed their wardrobes, accessories, hairstyles, and deliveries. I compared my performance with theirs. Finally one day the Lord whispered to me, "Cheryl, it's okay if you admire your colleagues, but in the process, don't diminish what I've placed in you or try to emulate them. I have one assignment for you: to pull out of *you* everything I've deposited in you. That's it. Focus on that."

And that is what God is saying to you. He has uniquely crafted you with specific gifts and abilities to accomplish certain things in life. You may have one gift or multiple abilities. In talking about the spiritual gifts, the apostle Paul said in 1 Corinthians 12:11 (NLT): "It is the one and only Spirit who distributes all these gifts. He alone decides which gift each person should have." He says later in 2 Corinthians 10:12 that it's useless for us to spend time comparing and measuring ourselves with each other. He calls it unwise. Instead, he says our goal should be to stay within the boundaries of God's plan for us. That's another way of saying concentrate on maximizing what God has equipped and called you to do.

When we compare, compete, and covet, we can't win because there is always someone else smarter, richer, more talented, or more beautiful than we are. Depression sets in. Never forget that you are a designer's original! Thank God for making you distinctively you; accept your package.

Psalm 16:5 says, "Lord, you alone are my portion and my cup; you make my lot secure." The *New Living Translation* says, "Lord . . . you guard all that is mine." That is very comforting, because it says that God has given each of us our assignment. He knows what we can handle, and what is for us is for us. It's secure.

This promise frees us to applaud the gifts, talent, beauty, and intellect of other women. I know it can be extremely difficult not to compare, compete, or covet if a guy you were secretly hoping to date or have dated starts dating another woman. Then you hear they are making marriage plans. This could cause you to go into deep depression or anger, and wonder, "What is it about her that made him want to marry her, and not me?"

That's actually the wrong question to ask. You may never get the answer, since decisions based on love are subjective. I believe we should return to what God's Word says about our destiny and remember that His plans for us are always

28

good. I've had to do this when guys I was interested in walked away. In retrospect, I have no regrets. I now thank God for every rejection. He was at work. I choose to remind myself of what Psalm 84:11 (NLT) says, and believe it: "The Lord will withhold no good thing from those who do what is right." Think about it this way: What if God caused the guy to lose interest in you to keep you on the path He ordained for you, and keep you from marrying the wrong person for you? After all, we can make one crucial decision that will totally change the course of our lives.

So what are you to do? Be distinct. Maximize the package you've been given. If you struggle in these areas, admit it to God and ask for His help. Don't be impressed with yourself. Don't compare yourself with others. When your life is over and you stand before God, His question to you will be this: "Did you complete the assignment I gave you? Did you maximize it?"

Comparing, competing, and coveting are equal-opportunity blockers. Peter suffered from them as well. In John 21, Jesus had just given Peter a preview of his life and death that would glorify Him. Then Jesus told Peter, "Follow me" (v. 19). As soon as Jesus said that, Peter immediately turned around and focused on the other disciple in Jesus' inner circle, John, and inquired about his fate. I believe Peter was secretly competitive with John. He had not dealt with this issue of the heart and his internal dialogue. "A good person produces good things from the treasury of a good heart. . . . What you say flows from what is in your heart" (Luke 6:45 NLT). But Jesus knew what was lodged in Peter's heart. He gave a very terse answer: "If I want him to remain alive until I return, what is that to you? As for you, follow me" (John 21:22 NLT). In today's language Jesus might have said, "What I am doing in John's life and what I have planned for him is none of your business, Peter. You concentrate on doing what I called you to do."

I admit that conquering the three C's is a continual battle. The age of social media intensifies the struggle. We now have access to the dreams, ambitions, and accomplishments of people around the globe. Of course, their websites, Facebook, and Twitter pages showcase the best and most exciting elements of their lives. The "commercials" are fantastic. It is so easy to see someone who does what you do and does it better or has more exciting opportunities, and think, *What about me? Why isn't my business or marriage flourishing? Their life is so wonderful compared to mine.* Don't believe the lie. I have made the mistake of doing this only to find out it was a mirage. When my eyes became open to the truth, I was angry at myself for all the time I wasted looking at the fairy-tale life of someone else who was actually living a nightmare or a life filled with challenges just like mine.

Now I stop myself when I'm about to revisit the fantasy life of a new victim. I try my best to train myself to think nothing about her life and how well it may be going. I practice praying for those who appear to be succeeding, asking God for their continued success and protection. I remind myself of John the Baptist's response when one of his disciples noted (in John 3) that the crowds were leaving them and following Jesus, though John had started his ministry first. John replied,

No one can receive anything unless God gives it from heaven. You yourselves know how plainly I told you, "I am not the Messiah. I am only here to prepare the way for him." It is the bridegroom who marries the bride, and the best man is simply glad to stand with him and hear his vows. Therefore, I am filled with joy at his success. He must become greater and greater, and I must become less and less.

John 3:27–30 NLT

I love John the Baptist's response. No sign of comparing his ministry with his cousin's, competing with Jesus for the crowds, or coveting Jesus' influence. Why? He knew his place: He was the usher, not the groom. He knew that it was God who gave each one his assignment without consulting them. John also knew who he was and who he was not. He was not deity. Jesus was. He came from earth. Jesus came from heaven. His understanding was limited. Jesus knew all things. John also knew his assignment (to prepare the way for Jesus) and his limitations. He was created to do just one thing in life: get people ready for Christ's arrival on the scene. No matter how long and hard he worked to accomplish his mission and expand his ministry, Jesus would *always* be greater. Always. In fact, John's influence would continually diminish the more Jesus' ministry flourished. John was never depressed about this reality because he was never in competition with Jesus. He said, "I am filled with joy at His success." He realized that God ordained that Jesus would be great. Jesus' greatness took nothing from John's distinctiveness.

When we stand before God, He'll only ask us about one assignment: the one He gave us.

Are you genuinely happy when those who do what you do are extremely successful and you are barely getting by and still toiling to make a name for yourself? You can be. I have read the John 3 passage over and over and fervently prayed that I will always be sincerely full of joy at the success of my friends and

31

colleagues. I have told myself repeatedly, "I refuse to compare, compete, or covet. This is my sister. We are on the same team. God called her like He called me. He ordained her to accomplish more for the kingdom of God than me. Her success in no way diminishes what God has called me to do. I will be judged by God based on the completion of my assignment." I remind myself that I am not to seek greatness. "Should you then seek great things for yourself? Do not seek them" (Jeremiah 45:5).

When Jesus got word that John the Baptist was in prison, he said, "Truly I tell you, among those born of women there has not risen anyone greater than John the Baptist" (Matthew 11:11).

Let's pledge to stop comparing, competing, and coveting, and only focus on doing our best to reach our maximum level of distinction, and let God do the rest. *Will you take the pledge with me?* When we stand before God, He'll only ask us about one assignment: the one He gave us.

becoming distinctly you

1. Describe your challenge of avoiding the three C's of comparing, competing, and coveting.

2. Who have you compared yourself with and why?

3. Which of the three C's have you found most challenging to conquer?

4. How can you apply what Jesus told Peter in John 21:15–22 to your own life?

5. Read John 3:27–30. What accounted for John the Baptist's lack of insecurity? What can you learn from him to help you overcome the three C's?

───── *Nugget* ─────

With God's help, make a pledge to stop comparing, competing, and coveting. If you are ready, read and sign this pledge:

I, _____, confess that I struggle with the Distinctly You blockers of comparing, competing, and coveting. I admit that conquering these three C's is an ongoing battle, especially _____. But by God's grace and strength and the power of His Word, I believe it is possible. I pledge today to end this practice so I can be free to be the woman God distinctly created me to be. I promise to immediately bring to the Lord and confess any feelings of inadequacy, jealousy, envy, or resentment as a result of comparing, competing, or coveting.

_____
Signed

_____
Date

4

A Small View of God

Sometimes I think we are more impressed with ourselves and others than we are with God. We forget how big He is and how very small we are. Did you know that from where God sits, He can check out everybody in the world at one glance? Everybody. That is the unfathomable power of the God we can know intimately.

I can tell if I have a momentarily small view of God based on what I *see,* what I *say,* what I *do,* and what I *think.* For example, if I see a situation as hopeless, I have a small view of God. Why? There is nothing God can't do. If I keep focusing on the "facts" of the case rather than exercising faith, then I have a small view of God because Christ followers "live by faith, not by sight" (2 Corinthians 5:7).

If words of doubt and negativity come out of my mouth, that's another clear sign that I'm not dependent on God, but independent. What we say is a powerful indicator of what we believe. I've discovered it's easy to talk faith. It's another thing to act in faith, to live it out every day, every hour, and to see only the bigness of God in every disappointing circumstance. Abraham failed this test when he fled to Egypt during a famine. He feared he would be killed if the Egyptians discovered the beautiful Sarah was his wife. His solution? He told her to lie about their relationship. "Please tell them you are my sister. Then they will spare my life and treat me well because of their interest in you" (Genesis 12:13 NLT). Sarah obeyed, and despite Abraham's small view of God in this instance, God in His mercy intervened and protected them both.

Some people live by the glass half-empty, never half-full rule. They possess a "yes-but" blocker instead of a "can-do" builder attitude. Remember the twelve men sent to investigate the Promised Land in Numbers 13? The question was not whether they could seize it (God had already guaranteed that) but what they would encounter. It was an exploration trek. Ten out of the twelve returned answering the wrong question, wrongly. They saw the inhabitants and freaked out with fear. They had quickly forgotten that God on your side always puts you in the majority. You are destined to win every battle His way. Their decision to see the glass half empty spread like wildfire. The comforting and confident words of Joshua and Caleb ("We should go up and take possession of the land, for we can certainly do it" [Numbers 13:30]) fell on deaf ears. The damage of a negative report had been done.

Regularly examine your thoughts and perceptions. Is your mind trained to think the worst and not the best, to see the obstacles, not the opportunities? It's not only pessimists who see the glass half empty, but also those who don't examine their thinking on a regular basis. The battle is in the mind. That's why

Christ followers are constantly encouraged to renew our minds daily. "Let God transform you into a new person by changing the way you think. Then you will learn to know God's will for you, which is good and pleasing and perfect" (Romans 12:2 NLT).

Is your thinking "stinking"? If so, it will block you from being distinct. Do you start your day with defeatist thoughts, beginning with *I can't; I don't have; I don't know why; I'm not?* If so, you will go downhill from there. Listen to your self-talk and change it immediately when it doesn't line up with the truths of God's Word. What are you thinking about when you're thinking? Do you see a bright future based on the promises of God? Do you see God as always above your circumstances? It's important to always live in the truth of God's Word moment by moment.

I've often heard single women lament the fact that there are no available single guys in their churches. They are bordering on depression because while their biological clocks are ticking, no prospects, only suspects, are knocking on their doors. My response is always, "Who says your church is the *only* and best place to meet your future mate?" Does not the omniscient God have the ultimate Rolodex? He knows where every single man in the universe lives. His timing is perfect, and so are His matchmaking skills. They were launched thousands of years before eHarmony and Match.com.

Negativity and looking out, not up, caused the ten spies to return with a negative report. They influenced an entire generation to miss their Promised Land. Don't let the same syndrome cause you to miss yours.

I remember when I was going through the worst saga of my life. My husband of three years walked away from our marriage with no desire for reconciliation. My hands were tied. Crying out to God intensely and to my husband for reconciliation was not changing his mind or the outcome. I was consumed daily with a drama sizzling hot enough for a Hollywood movie. I could think of nothing else. Finally one morning, the Lord spoke to me and said, "Cheryl, Cheryl, have you forgotten that I am *sovereign*? I am the *same* God who parted the Red Sea for Moses. I am the *same* God who can move mountains. Get a grip. Don't you think I can stop this charade anytime I want? No one can thwart my purposes. No one can stop me from being God. Your focus has been in the wrong place. You need to be consumed with *me*. I am always in charge of all things. Nothing catches me by surprise."

"I am the same God who parted the Red Sea for Moses. I am the same God who can move mountains."

That reminder stopped me in my tracks. I was limiting God. What could I say but acknowledge the truth that the God I serve is sovereign. *Sovereign* means "having supreme rank, power, or authority; being above all others in character, importance, excellence." From that day forward, I viewed my circumstances differently. The drama didn't end immediately, but I was confident that God was still on my side, He would never fail me, and it would ultimately end up for my good. No, the ending was not the storybook happily ever after, but instead a story of God healing my broken heart and all the scars of rejection over time. It is a story confirming God's promises that when we go through the water and the fire He will be with us (Isaiah 43:2). It may not be good or feel good, but when God gets through, good comes out of the trial, the disappointment.

Resist having a small view of God. Reflect on His ability to do the impossible. Remember that nothing and no one can thwart His purposes and that He is committed to bringing out your distinctiveness for His glory. Change your view of God and you will flourish.

becoming distinctly **you**

1. Describe your view of God today.
2. When has what you said, saw, did, or thought revealed your small view of God?
3. How has a small view of God blocked your distinctiveness?
4. Are you prone to think the worst or the best? To see obstacles or opportunities? Why?
5. What is your constant self-talk about God?
6. What do you need to do to maintain a proper view of God?

~ *Nugget* ~

Review Romans 12:2. Be willing to cooperate with God and let Him transform your thinking so He is never small in your eyes.

5

A Large View of Yourself

Just as bad as having a small view of God is having a large (oversized) view of yourself. It's called pride. An *I* is in the middle. The Bible has much to say about pride, and none of it is good. Here are some examples: "The Lord hates . . . a proud look"; "By pride comes nothing but strife" (Proverbs 6:16–17; 13:10 NKJV). We can never be distinctive God's way when we are full of ourselves. God esteems those who are humble in heart, and who recognize their ultimate dependency on Him at all times. This is totally opposite from what the culture tells us. We are encouraged to flaunt what we have and let others know how wonderful we are, because if we don't, no one else will. Some live and die by the motto "It's all about me!" No, it's all about God and His will for our lives.

I pray constantly that the Lord will remove every ounce of pride that may be lurking in the recesses of my heart. The circumstances of life can cause pride to rear its ugly head. For example: You did not get the promotion you knew you deserved. The fact that you *thought* you deserved it is a sign of pride. (I know, because God had to correct me on this one.) You look around at certain married women, and in your heart you can't figure out why *they* are married and not you. You do the once-over, and you clearly eclipse them in every way, two to one. This is a big sign of pride.

You find yourself name-dropping in hopes that others will be impressed. *Pride.* You take credit for all your accomplishments. After all, you pulled yourself up by your *own* bootstraps. God is never acknowledged as the source of your intellect, good fortune, looks, talent, boots, or straps. Proverbs 16:18 (NKJV) says, "Pride goes before destruction, and a haughty spirit before a fall." Pride can be deadly.

Pride blocks us from being distinctive from God's point of view. How can we tap into His plan for creating us if we have our own agenda mapped out, are opposed to knowing Him, and are committed to going our own way?

How can we tap into His plan for creating us if we have our own agenda mapped out?

The great army commander Naaman, highly regarded by his peers, almost missed his healing because of pride. His story is told in 2 Kings 5. Naaman was successful, but he had a big problem. He had leprosy. Like AIDS today, leprosy was incurable. His wife's servant girl (from Israel) said to her mistress, "If only my master would see the prophet who is in Samaria! He would cure him of his leprosy" (2 Kings 5:3).

Naaman decided to give it a try. What did he have to lose? But Naaman's expectations were not met when he traveled to

Elisha's house. Elisha did not come out to greet him, but instead sent a messenger. Elisha's action insulted Naaman. Because of his position, he was expecting the royal treatment. Naaman also disliked the instructions given: "Go, wash yourself seven times in the Jordan, and your flesh will be restored and you will be cleansed" (2 Kings 5:10). The Jordan was a small, dirty river. In Naaman's mind, dipping into this body of water was beneath him. He couldn't get past the instructions. Naaman went away angry:

> "I thought that he would surely come out to me and stand and call on the name of the Lord his God, wave his hand over the spot and cure me of my leprosy. Are not Abana and Pharpar, the rivers of Damascus, better than all the waters of Israel? Couldn't I wash in them and be cleansed?" So he turned and went off in a rage.
>
> 2 Kings 5:11–12

Can you identify with Naaman? I can. You have an urgent, specific need. You've cried out to God, expecting Him to answer. You prayed specifically. The only thing is His answer is not what you had in mind. First, Elisha sent a messenger with healing instructions for Naaman. That surprised Naaman, given his position. Then he thought Elisha would engage in a prayer session with him, call on the name of the Lord, wave his hand over the spot, and cure him of leprosy. He had probably rehearsed this scene many times in his mind. Instead, Elisha's healing instructions were unthinkable to Naaman: Wash seven times in the dirty Jordan River. Fortunately, Naaman's servants convinced him to "just do it." After all, what could he possibly lose but his pride and dignity? He complied, and was completely cleansed of the leprosy.

41

God used my failed marriage to reveal the leprosy in my heart. It was not physical but spiritual. I didn't sign up for divorce or dream about it when I was a little girl. My only fantasy was a great marriage with a great man of God. What good came out of my brokenness and my disappointment? When my ears finally stopped buzzing so I could hear what God was saying to me, about me (not my husband), He said, "Cheryl, I want you to put your spiritual pride on the altar, because that's what you are full of right now."

At first, I was shocked. Me? Spiritual pride? The answer was yes. I hadn't realized that I was spiritually smug, because I had accepted Christ as my Lord and Savior when I was a child. I hadn't committed any really big sins. My prayers were typically answered the way I wanted. I was an achiever, got into the best schools, and got hired by NBC News right out of graduate school. I assumed all these wonderful things happened because of *my* walk with the Lord. Bad things happened to other people because they weren't walking with the Lord or didn't have the depth of relationship that I had with the Lord.

How prideful was that viewpoint? As my father used to say often, "Some people are proud and don't know it." That was me. But God knew. He knew that crud needed to be exposed and expunged. The death of my marriage did it. I had inwardly harshly judged other Christians with failed marriages without knowing all the facts, or any facts. I was brought up hearing that "God hates divorce," and you simply don't get one, period. Not once did it occur to me that there is no choice when someone no longer wants you and walks away. You are a victim of divorce whether you want to be or not. That's where I was. All of my judgmental thoughts about others came back on me. I was traumatized by the fact that other believers could be talking about me behind my back the way I once talked about others going through the pain of divorce. They didn't know the facts like I did. They just knew that my marriage had failed.

Jesus once again pointed out my pride, my smugness, and said, "Put it on the altar so the dross can be consumed. I can't use you the way I want to use you with this pride and sense of entitlement running rampant." Before the Lord spoke, I had assumed that all the lessons were for my mate and I was an innocent player in the drama. Not so. God wastes no experience. When I put my spiritual pride on the altar, my eyes opened. I saw myself as I really was: a woman with absolutely no righteousness of her own, only a recipient of God's grace. For the first time I realized that all that I had, all that I was, every door that opened in my life was because of one thing: God's wonderful grace. That's it. All of my righteousness was as filthy rags. I was not entitled to anything on my own. An attitude of entitlement stinks in God's nostrils.

We are prone to evaluate success or failure based on our view of ourselves. We judge others when they are struggling with health, loss, poverty, or disappointment. We secretly blame them for making poor choices and put ourselves and our "wisdom" on a pedestal. We think, *My life is turning out well because I've made great choices; theirs is a mess because of the poor choices they've made.* How many parents experience bouts of depression because they reared their children in a God-honoring way, yet the children chose to take the wayward path? They forget that we all have a free will, and their children's choices in no way reflect on their child-rearing. Think about it. God placed Adam and Eve in a perfect environment, exceeding all their expectations. They lacked nothing. Yet they chose to disobey God, knowing the consequences of their actions. Their disobedience was no reflection on God. It was their choice, and their choice caused God to keep His promise of dire consequences.

I couldn't change my mate's choice to leave, but I could choose my response: to humble myself before God and ask Him to change my heart and remove everything in it that displeased Him. God lovingly purged me from that awful spiritual pride and changed me to see every good thing in my life simply as His grace, not my goodness. God's work in me has been transformative. Now, I never go around thinking, *I deserve this*, or *Of course, this should happen to me*. Instead, when a great opportunity comes my way or when I'm asked to speak on God's behalf, gratitude overwhelms me that God would use an imperfect vessel to declare His perfect truth. He has given me the privilege of being on His team despite my imperfections and sins. It is always Him at work in me. It is never about me.

Want to impress God? Drop the pride.

I remember one day when I was walking out my door, reflecting on my life and all the great things that had happened, and I said, "God, I can clearly point to you as the source of these wonderful things. But what do I say when I get to the big *D*: divorce? What's the answer there?" Immediately I heard Him say, "That's when you tell them about my grace."

Want to impress God? Drop the pride. Replace it with humility. "These are the ones I look on with favor: those who are humble and contrite in spirit, and who tremble at my word" (Isaiah 66:2). Do you want to be esteemed by your friends, your co-workers, and the culture—or by God? He delights in those who are humble in heart, who refuse to second-guess

Him, who see their need for Him, who long to please Him, and who just obey.

becoming distinctly you

1. How can you spot pride in your life?
2. How do you know pride is a factor in your self-talk, your decisions, and your conversations?
3. Have you ever been guilty of name-dropping or bragging or using the word *I* too many times? If so, did the Holy Spirit convict you? What did these actions reveal about what was going on in your heart?
4. Discuss how Naaman almost missed out on a miracle because of his pride.
5. What are the lessons you can learn from Naaman?

6

Fickle Feelings

Feelings are fickle. One day you love your job; the next day you hate it. During Sunday worship you're convinced you can conquer anything; by the time you walk to your car, you're overwhelmed with feelings of despair. Just like that you're back to square one, riding either the roller coaster or the seesaw called feelings. A. R. Bernard says, "Human emotions are highly variable, decidedly unpredictable, and often unreliable."[1]

Our feelings or emotions can't be trusted, yet so many people make major decisions based on a feeling or a gut reaction. I know. I've been guilty of making a rash judgment about someone or something based on feelings, not facts. I've run with an idea that simply popped into my head out of nowhere. One time I was on my knees praying with my mind on the Lord, and this thought came in looming large: *Richard (that's the name I'll give him), is the godly man you've been waiting for.* I stopped praying and thought, *Richard? Richard??? Can this be true? He doesn't even like me, not in that way. We're friends, but it's only a platonic relationship.* This impression caught me off guard and stumped my prayer session. I analyzed it and pondered it for days. I asked, "Was this God speaking, Cheryl speaking, or someone else?" I was not attracted to Richard, but I was willing to obey God if this was His will. Over time it was obvious that this "revelation" was false; Richard was never interested in me, and he married someone else. My "unction" was totally off base. I'm so glad I didn't share my "revelation" with Richard or with other friends.

Feelings should only be trusted when they are confirmed by God's Word. We are to be ruled by faith and obedience to God, not our feelings. This is a great challenge because everything in our culture encourages us to live by our instinct, our gut. We're told to "go with your feelings, go with your heart. Do what you think is best." People have walked away from their spouse, or their job when they didn't have another one and were deep in debt, bought new luxury cars and designer purses they could not afford, all because of *feelings*.

Feelings can derail or delay your destiny. We can be full of faith one minute, and guided by feelings the next. Satan uses them to short-circuit the perfect plan of God in our lives. Remember when God told Abraham that he would become the father of many nations, and that Sarah would give birth to a son even though she was barren? They were both past their prime, but God said, "'A son who is your own flesh and blood will be your heir. . . . Look up at the sky and count the stars—if indeed you can count them.' Then he said to him, 'So shall your offspring be.' Abram believed the Lord" (Genesis 15:4–6).

Abraham stood firm in his faith initially, but then God did not produce a child on his and Sarah's timetable. It was taking much longer than they had expected. They were already old when they received the promise, and they were only getting older, making the prospect even more inconceivable. Then Sarah's mind started twirling: *Maybe God meant something else. Maybe He expects us to use our common sense, get proactive, and help Him out.* So Sarah hatched the idea of her husband sleeping with their young Egyptian maidservant, Hagar. She would be the surrogate. They would have their baby. Based on Sarah's feelings at the time, it made perfect sense. After all, she said, "The Lord has kept me from having children. Go, sleep with my slave; perhaps I can build a family through her" (Genesis 16:2). The plan worked, except it wasn't God's plan.

Before you cast a judgmental eye at Sarah, reflect on your life and past decisions. How many times have you moved ahead of God simply because you got tired of waiting for Him to act? You were led by your emotions, and they told you it's taking too long for the right job to come along, the right man to come into your life, for the children you desperately desire. You've prayed and prayed and prayed, but God is not in a hurry. So you got busy. I'm guilty as charged. There were times when I got ahead of God. Like Sarah, because of a delay (God is never on our time schedule), I began to wonder, "Maybe I didn't really hear from God about this. Maybe I'm supposed to do something to bring the desired results. After all, He did make me an intelligent woman, and I should use my brain and do something. Wouldn't He expect me to do that?" Added to the fuel is the pressure from the culture to create your own opportunities, chart your own path, make a splash, and get noticed.

The only thing is I don't find this strategy in God's Word. We are told to

> Hold tightly without wavering to the hope we affirm, for God can be trusted to keep his promise. . . . So do not throw away this confident trust in the Lord. Remember the great reward it brings you! Patient endurance is what you need now, so that you will continue to do God's will. Then you will receive all that he has promised.
>
> Hebrews 10:23, 35–36 NLT

When we get busy and concoct a deliverance of our own based on our feelings and reasoning, this indicates we don't trust God and we have more confidence in our own schemes. It seems like a great idea at the time, but once it's hatched, it creates havoc. Ask Sarah. Yes, Hagar conceived a son, but he was not the child God promised. Chaos and crisis followed. We sometimes think that God will stop us from making a colossal mistake, and if He doesn't, then He's okay with it. I heard apologist and author Ravi Zacharias say, "If you are determined in going a certain direction, God will step aside and second your motion."[2] In other words, He will not violate our free will. How dare we get mad at God because He didn't stop us from doing what *we* wanted to do? He has spoken loudly through His Word. It alone is our guiding light.

I learned this the hard way. A nice Christian man expressed interest in me and began to pursue a relationship. I had learned to inquire of God on the front end. When we were planning the first date, I had a strong unction that I should graciously say no. I didn't know why, since he passed the first test of being a man who was pursuing God. I ignored this prompting and we moved forward. As a result of circumstances out of his control, the date had to be postponed. I was actually relieved because of that initial uneasiness. But unfortunately, I did not close the door to future opportunities. Why? I liked him and was attracted to him. The second date we arranged was not canceled. After a few weeks of communicating, I still could not shake the inner prompting that this relationship was not God's will. I decided to obey God and bring it to a halt. But I made a crucial mistake. I shared my decision (before executing it) with a trusted friend. She had never met "Bob," and when she did, she said, "I can't believe you're going to let him get away." I forgot what God said and went with what *she* said. Bad move. My heart was never at peace during the relationship. I went with my feelings, my desires, and poor counsel, and it almost ended in matrimony, except for God's amazing grace.

At least I had learned one important lesson, and that is, despite my feelings, I must always cry out to God intensely for His will, not mine. So daily (while dating), I was crying out to God to make His will clear. Even though I thought I loved Bob and we were contemplating marriage, I truly wanted God's will more than I wanted my way. I kept "asking, seeking, and knocking." I knew that my feelings were fickle and not to be trusted. When you want what you want when you want it, it's hard to discern God's voice.

It took a while to empty myself of Cheryl's desires so I could hear God clearly. I logged many hours praying, asking God to reveal His will in a way that I would clearly understand. I just didn't want to miss it. Sure enough, God came through on a day I least expected and made it extremely clear that this relationship was not His will. It dissolved immediately through a series of unexpected circumstances. I thanked God profusely. Bob was a good man, a godly man, but not God's choice for me.

His peace enveloped my soul. Joy overwhelmed me. Later, the Lord spoke to me and said, "Cheryl, I want to make one thing clear: I didn't answer your prayer because *you* are all that. You're not. I answered your prayer in the nick of time because you had sense enough to do one thing: You kept asking, seeking, and knocking, which is what you're commanded to do. I answered your prayer because I am always obligated to honor my Word. Always."

I learned a valuable lesson as a result of this ordeal. We are encouraged to seek godly counsel when we are unsure of the best course of action. "In the multitude of counselors there is safety" (Proverbs 11:14 NKJV). But when God has clearly spoken, no other counsel is needed. The next step is ACTION. I made a strategic mistake when I did not immediately obey God's prompting to end the relationship. I valued what my friend said over God's clear direction.

What if Abraham had consulted with Sarah after God specifically told him, "Take your son, your only son, whom you love—Isaac—and go to the region of Moriah. Sacrifice him there as a burnt offering on a mountain I will show you" (Genesis 22:2)? I don't think Abraham would have made it to the mountain at all or without an intense argument with his wife.

You can't trust your feelings, but you can always trust God.

It would probably go something like this: "Abraham, are you sure you heard from God? I don't believe it! It doesn't make any sense. We waited all these years for God to give us a son. God made it clear nations would come through Isaac. So why would God then ask you to kill him? I'm sorry, Abraham, I can't go along with this. You are not taking my son anywhere!"

For good reason, Abraham conferred with no one. God had spoken. "Early the next morning Abraham got up and loaded his donkey. He took with him two of his servants and his son Isaac. When he had cut enough wood for the burnt offering, he set out for the place God had told him about" (Genesis 22:3). Abraham responded without delay to the call of God. He left the consequences of his obedience to God. God provided a sacrificial ram in the bush.

Avoid Isolation

Another fickle feeling is a desire to isolate ourselves from others. We can never be our best living in isolation. God created us for community, not to be alone. "Iron sharpens iron" (Proverbs 27:17). He uses other people in our lives to provide encouragement and wise, godly counsel. A sense of despair and discouragement can precede isolation. Just ask the great prophet Elijah. He had just called fire down from heaven, putting God's power on display. He prayed,

> Lord, the God of Abraham, Isaac and Israel, let it be known today that you are God in Israel and that I am your servant and have done all these things at your command. Answer me, Lord, answer me, so these people will know that you, Lord, are God, and that you are turning their hearts back again.
>
> 1 Kings 18:36–37

God answered Elijah and fire fell from heaven and burned up the sacrifice, the wood, the stones, and the soil. After this display of God's awesome power, the people fell prostrate and cried that the Lord, He is God!

You would think Elijah would be basking for days in the glow of this miracle and that he would forever be unshakable in his faith. Not so. A threat from Queen Jezebel left him fearful. After she heard what Elijah had done and how he killed all the prophets of Baal with a sword, she sent this message to Elijah: "May the gods deal with me, be it ever so severely, if by this time tomorrow I do not make your life like that of one of them" (1 Kings 19:2). What was his response? "Elijah was afraid and ran for his life" (1 Kings 19:3). He left town, went into the desert, and prayed to die. He wasn't thinking straight. He continued his journey alone and was on the run for forty days and nights.

Dr. Charles Stanley says to always remember H.A.L.T: Don't get too hungry, angry, lonely, or tired. Elijah was all four. God fed him in the desert, and afterward he fell asleep. No one was there to encourage him, so God stepped in. One day He asked him, "What are you doing here, Elijah?" (1 Kings 19:9). Elijah told God about the death threat and that he was the last prophet standing. He was wrong.

It's easy to lose the proper perspective of our predicament when we take our eyes off of God and His promises, and instead concentrate on the present situation. God promises to be our helper and to never leave us or forsake us. He says in effect, "If I am for you, I am more than the whole world against you" (see Romans 8:31). Elijah forgot and we forget. We can only see our pain, disappointment, and rejection. We go into the "woe is me" mode. Isolation only intensifies these feelings because we have no one to encourage us and bring us back to reality.

God in His compassion and love told Elijah, "Go out and stand on the mountain in the presence of the Lord, for the Lord is about to pass by" (1 Kings 19:11). A powerful wind, an earthquake, and a fire appeared. God was not in them. He came through a gentle whisper. God asked Elijah, "What are you doing here, Elijah?" (1 Kings 19:13). He repeated the same story of being God's servant, doing his will, and now being the only prophet left, running for his life to avoid the bounty on his head.

God told him to return home and anoint Elisha to succeed him as prophet. He would have a close friend to share life's triumphs and struggles. God also corrected Elijah's analysis of being the only person left who was true to God. "Yet I reserve seven thousand in Israel—all whose knees have not bowed down to Baal and all whose mouths have not kissed him" (1 Kings 19:18).

Isolation can lead to self-pity and unhealthy introspection. Sometimes it is forced on us by circumstances beyond our control. We're pushed out of a job, a marriage, or an unhealthy relationship. That was Hagar's story. She was forced to have sex with her master, Abraham, in order to produce an heir, since Sarah was barren. After she produced the child, Sarah was jealous. After Sarah gave birth to Isaac, Hagar's son Ishmael mocked his younger brother. That's when Sarah had enough and demanded that Abraham get rid of Hagar and her son. Abraham complied. They went on their way, wandering in the desert. They were alone and out of water. Hagar cried, thinking this was the end for her and her son. But God was watching and listening.

The angel of God called to Hagar from heaven and said to her, "What is the matter, Hagar? Do not be afraid; God has heard the boy crying as he lies there. Lift the boy up and take him by the hand, for I will make him into a great nation." Then God opened her eyes and she saw a well of water. So she went and filled the skin with water and gave the boy a drink.

Genesis 21:17–19

No matter how desperate our situation, God is always with us. He is aware of every tear and heartbreak. His presence brought Hagar peace, provision, and a promise. Hagar and Ishmael were considered outcasts, but not by God. He still had great plans for them. And God always has great plans for us, if we trust and never doubt, no matter how desolate our situation appears to be.

Satan loves to get us isolated from everyone so he can whisper his lies in our ears. I remember when my husband left me; I faced a mental battle every day. It was the same devastating pronouncement: *God cannot use you anymore; your testimony is shot, and you will never marry again. You're used goods. Why would a godly man choose you when there are so many women available who have never married? It's over for you!* It was taunting and tormenting. I didn't want to get out of bed, I felt so bad. Like Hagar, someone else's choice determined my fate as an outcast. I was depressed and despondent. Fortunately, my mother, my brother Jerry, and my sister-in-love Jackie kept tabs on me and called regularly.

I was so drained emotionally and physically that I had stopped my regimen of seeking God daily. I was just trying to survive moment by moment. Satan attacks us when we are most vulnerable. One day I decided to return to my spiritual nourishment. I began reading my Bible again. I found myself getting stronger each day. I started sleeping with my Bible. God's Word was my lifeline once again.

Beware of Anger

Unresolved anger will also derail your distinctiveness. It can eat away like a cancer. We are unable to move forward and be all that God wants us to be when our hearts are full of anger. It manifests itself in our speech, our eyes, and our body language. We can be on the rampage to ruin reputations when our heart is blocked with anger.

We are unable to move forward and be all that God wants us to be when our hearts are full of anger.

Esau had a justifiable reason to be angry at his twin brother, Jacob. Jacob had taken advantage of Esau twice. Jacob was cooking some stew one day, when Esau came home famished. He thought he was near death unless he got something to eat quickly. He asked Jacob for some of his stew. Jacob offered it under one condition: Esau had to sell him his birthright. This was a special honor designated to the firstborn son. He was guaranteed the position of family leader at the appropriate time. He would receive a double portion of the family inheritance. Esau was so shortsighted in the moment that he agreed to sell his birthright for a bowl of stew.

Later, when their father was old and blind, Esau experienced the ultimate deception from his brother and mother, Rebekah. She was determined that her favorite, Jacob, would receive his father's blessing. She overheard Isaac tell Esau to go hunt some wild game for him and prepare it, then he would give him his blessing before he died.

Rebekah quickly rounded up Jacob to go fetch two goats so she could prepare the meal while Esau was away. She put

Esau's clothes on Jacob and added some goatskins on his arms to make him hairy like his older brother. The scheme worked. Jacob lied to his father and said he was Esau. Isaac was suspicious initially, but was eventually convinced enough to extend the double-portion blessing to Jacob.

When Esau returned from his hunting expedition, he found out he had been duped once again. "Esau held a grudge against Jacob because of the blessing his father had given him. He said to himself, 'The days of mourning for my father are near; then I will kill my brother Jacob'" (Genesis 27:41).

Seething with anger, Esau could think of no alternative but murder. Fortunately, over a long period of time, his heart softened and love returned for his brother. You never know what you are capable of thinking or doing when your anger is out of control. I remember when I went through my marital ordeal, my feelings fluctuated. One moment I was okay, the next, I was boiling with anger. I pulled out my victim card: "After all I've done for this marriage, all the sacrifices I've made, I can't believe this is what I get in return!"

One day God set me straight about this. He said, "Don't ever again bring up all the great things you did. Whatever you do for a person should be done unto me as an offering. You should expect nothing in return." Ouch. I never forgot that chastisement.

Jesus is our perfect example. He had every right to be angry, being thrust on a cross with nails in His hands and feet, having had a perfect record. There was no fault in Him. Yet He chose not to respond to His critics. He stopped dying long enough to promise heaven as a reward to the thief on the cross next to Him. He prayed to His father to forgive His accusers because they didn't know what they were doing. Jesus suffered at the hands of His enemies with no malice in His heart.

What's in your heart? What's there will determine what you think, how you act, and what you say. Proverbs 4:23 says, "Keep thy heart with all diligence; for out of it are the issues of life" (KJV). We safeguard and protect what's valuable to us. Our money is in the bank. Our cars and homes have alarm systems. But more important than guarding our money, cars, and homes is diligently guarding our hearts. Whatever is lodged there affects and controls everything we do. Hannah Whitall Smith says,

> Anything allowed in the heart which is contrary to the will of God, let it seem ever so insignificant, or be ever so deeply hidden, will cause us to fall before our enemies. Any root of bitterness cherished towards another, any self-seeking, any harsh judgments indulged in, any slackness in obeying the voice of the Lord, any doubtful habits . . . any one of these things will effectually cripple and paralyze our spiritual life.[3]

This is why regularly monitoring our hearts is crucial. It is the key to a healthy, whole relationship with God and with others. What if Esau had taken his complaints about his brother directly to God? What if he had taken responsibility for the role he played in his demise by agreeing to sell his birthright? What if he had cried out to God to create in him a clean heart and remove all anger and bitterness toward his brother? The outcome would have been different. It always is when we take full responsibility for what we can do instead of being consumed with the other person's egregious sins.

Colossians 3:13 says, "You must make allowance for each other's faults and forgive the person who offends you. Remember, the Lord forgave you, so you must forgive others." The antidote to unresolved anger is to do what you can do and that is to forgive, whether the other person ever acknowledges the wrong. It's a commandment, not an option. God is able to release us from all anger and replace it with unconditional love for our enemies. We must desire this more than anything; talk to Him first (being transparent about our complaints) and then watch Him dissolve what has been handed to Him.

The Power of Fear

Fear is a feeling that paralyzes. You are filled with dreams and desires for your life, but fear is also in the equation. You can't move forward. Fear looms large. It's overpowering. What are you fearing? Inadequacy? Lack of education or knowledge? Not being smart enough? Not getting the money for the venture if you take that step of faith? Not being good enough? Not being pretty enough? That your network is too small or nonexistent? That a relationship you really desire won't work out?

Fear is a by-product of focusing on ourselves rather than on God's promises, on the obstacles, not the God-given opportunities. We are consumed with all the data about us (and it's not looking good), not the résumé of the God we serve. He controls all things. By Him, all things exist. He spoke this world into existence. No do-over was necessary on anything. He never makes a mistake. The nations of the world are like a drop in the bucket to Him. This God is the same God orchestrating your life for His purposes.

For years I had a terrible habit of becoming fearful whenever I was given an unexpected career opportunity. I am a planner, so when I was needed to fill in for an anchor or host at the last minute, I panicked. "What if I mess up? What if I don't have adequate time to prepare?" I learned to overcome this paralyzing fear by reminding myself that God was with me and He orchestrated the opportunity; therefore, He would give me everything I needed to excel. If I did all I could do in preparation, He would do what I could not do, which is give me clarity of thought and speech. In each assignment, I sensed His guidance. Now whenever I'm presented with opportunities, it's a habit to immediately acknowledge the Lord and remain confident that with His help, I can handle it.

Fear is a by-product of focusing on ourselves rather than on God's promises.

Barak did not have this inner assurance and, unfortunately, missed out on a great opportunity to be used by God. He was a top military general. One day Deborah, the judge, sent for him and said, "The Lord, the God of Israel, commands you: 'Go, take with you ten thousand men . . . and lead them up to Mount Tabor. I will lead Sisera, the commander of Jabin's army, with his chariots and his troops to the Kishon River and give him into your hands'" (Judges 4:6–7).

This was a direct promise from God, and Deborah delivered it perfectly to Barak. He heard what she said, but he was fearful. He wanted her to go with him. He said to her, "If you go with me, I will go; but if you don't go with me, I won't go" (Judges 4:8). Deborah responded with what God said: "Certainly I will go with you. But because of the course you are taking, the honor will not be yours, for the Lord will deliver Sisera into the hands of a woman" (Judges 4:9).

Deborah went with Barak, and just as God said, Barak pursued the chariots and army and succeeded. But the commander, Sisera, was killed when Ja-el, a woman, drove a peg through his temple.

I would hate for paralyzing fear to cause you and me to miss out on God's Plan A. Let's fight any fear lurking around with the shield of faith, confident that if God gives the assignment, He'll provide the means for victory.

Remember that fickle feelings are no respecter of persons. They overcame the "father of faith," destroyed sibling unity, derailed an influential prophet, and can wreak havoc on regular people like you and me. They run the gamut and can quickly overwhelm our reasoning and actions. If you are determined to walk the distinct path God tailor-made for you, it is essential to be guided by faith and not by your feelings, emotions, or desires. You can't trust your feelings, but you can always trust God. Every command is backed by a guarantee that His will is good, acceptable, and perfect. Why accept anything less?

Don't let feelings rule. Pull out your "sword of the Spirit, which is the word of God" (Ephesians 6:17). With this weapon you will defeat this Distinctly You blocker every time.

becoming distinctly you

1. Name a time your gut feeling or instinct led you to make a wrong decision or judgment about a person.

2. Have you ever been guilty of moving ahead of God because you grew tired of waiting for Him to act? If so, what was the outcome?

3. How can strong feelings obscure God's will?

4. What is the danger of isolation and seclusion?

5. Discuss the value of close friends on your road to becoming distinctly you.

6. Are you living with any unresolved anger? What do you need to do to discard it?

7. Consider a time when you were paralyzed by fear. What did you fear? How did you overcome it?

7

Distractions

I was so excited about getting my first car. I bought the silver Toyota Celica from my oldest brother, Truman. It was only a year old. The timing was perfect. I had just finished graduate school and was moving from Chicago to Washington to start a job at the NBC-owned television station.

I'd had the car for about two weeks when I had my first accident. I was driving along a street near my apartment, with the windows down, when a bee flew in. I panicked. I'm allergic to bee stings. I was determined to get that bee out of my car, and fast. I was an inexperienced driver, only getting my license right before I got the car. I took my eyes off the road to conquer that bee, and I crashed into the car in front of me. I did more damage to my car than his. Fortunately, no one was hurt.

I allowed a tiny bee to divert my attention. The results could have been deadly. That's all it usually takes, one distraction to take us off course from our distinct God-path. It can come suddenly, catching us off guard. I know, because I constantly battle distractions internally and externally. Distractions can be people, places, things, or thoughts. They are tailor-made, suited for our bent. The devil is the mastermind behind our distractions.

Ask King David. He was in the wrong place at the wrong time when a very beautiful woman got his attention. From his roof, David saw Bathsheba bathing. He wasn't supposed to be on his roof; he was supposed to be in battle with his army. But this time he decided to stay in Jerusalem. That's when he got in trouble, distracted by extreme beauty. The first glance was probably innocent; he was just looking over the landscape from his roof. But his looking turned to lusting and he had to have her. *Now.* All reasoning went out the window. The man David sent to find out about this mystery woman described her as "the wife of Uriah the Hittite" (2 Samuel 11:3). In other words, "King, she's taken. She's a married woman." David was too distracted and too determined to heed the hint. In the very next verse, he sent messengers to get her. "She came to him, and he slept with her" (2 Samuel 11:4).

The consequences of the distraction were enormous: adultery, a pregnancy, and murder. David's reputation with God had been stellar up to this point. God handpicked him to replace King Saul. He won every battle, had unprecedented success as king. And then one glance and one longing that turned into lust and was acted upon produced death—the death of an innocent man, Bathsheba's husband, Uriah (whom David had moved to the front lines of battle as part of the cover-up), and the death of his newborn child (God's punishment).

Another deadly distraction to be on guard against is our imagination. I call it "imagination gone wild." I have a vivid imagination. It doesn't take me long to go into fantasy mode about any and everything: a job, a date, a vacation, or a dining experience at a new restaurant. At times I create mental scenarios that are outstanding, almost unbelievable. Of course, the reality doesn't measure up because it was a fantasy. There have been times I thought a guy was interested in me simply because we had one decent conversation. I took the talk and turned it into a sign of a potential relationship. I entered Fantasyland. I was wrong. Other times, I've been automatically suspicious, thinking the worst, not the best, questioning someone's motives or behavior. I've learned that just because I think it, doesn't mean I have to say it or that it's true.

I encourage you to persevere to discard all those vain imaginations. Second Corinthians 10:5 commands us to "take captive every thought to make it obedient to Christ." It says *every* thought, and that requires discipline and concentration. It means always asking the question "Does this thought line up with what God's Word says?" If not, reject it and delete it immediately. Oswald Chambers says, "If you have been bringing every thought into captivity to the obedience of Christ, it will be one of the greatest assets to faith when the time of trial comes, because your faith and the Spirit of God will work together."[1]

Another way to look at it is "restraining the imagination." My favorite devotional, *Daily Strength for Daily Needs*, offers these wise words written many years ago by Jean N. Grou:

> There is another kind of silence to be cultivated, besides that of the tongue as regards others. I mean silence as regards one's self,—restraining the imagination, not permitting it to dwell overmuch on what we have heard or said, not indulging in [daydreaming], whether of the past or future. Be sure that

you have made no small progress in the spiritual life when you can control your imagination so as to fix it on the duty and occupation actually existing, to the exclusion of the crowd of thoughts, which are perpetually sweeping across the mind. No doubt, you cannot prevent those thoughts from arising, but you can prevent yourself from dwelling on them; you can put them aside, you can check the self-complacency, or irritation, or earthly longings that feed them, and by the practice of such control of your thoughts you will attain that spirit of inward silence that draws the soul into a close [fellowship] with God.[2]

It's best to think nothing until we have the facts. You've probably heard the adage that most of the things we think about never come to pass anyway. Isaiah 26:3 says, "Thou wilt keep him in perfect peace, whose [imagination] is stayed on thee" (KJV). Do you want the peace of God always guarding your heart and your mind? Keep your imagination (your mind, your fantasies, your thoughts) parked on Him. You won't have room to entertain distractions.

Adam and Eve hadn't been around long before Satan showed up to distract them from God's best plan. In Genesis 2:16–17, God commanded, "You are free to eat from any tree in the garden; but you must not eat from the tree of the knowledge of good and evil, for when you eat from it you will certainly die." This was not a complex mandate, but simple and easy to understand: You have free range to eat from any of the trees, except for one. If you choose to eat from that one, you will die. Rather than focusing on all that was available and within the realm of possibility, Eve, like us, became distracted with what she couldn't have. She had access to many trees but became fixated on the one that was off-limits. She knew what God said, but the devil countered with a half-truth: "You will not certainly die. . . . For

66

God knows that when you eat from it your eyes will be opened, and you will be like God, knowing good and evil" (Genesis 3:4–5). It was a strong, appealing argument ("You will be like God"), but wrong, because it defied what God said. This is why it's so important to decide on the front end that God's Word will always be your guide. It's the most direct route for blossoming into the person God called us to be. The minute we start thinking and reasoning about something God has already spoken on, we're headed for Trouble Lane. This is easy to do when we get caught up in our own intellect, perspective, or knowledge. We can enjoy the process of intelligent debate, but when God has spoken, there is no room for debate. God's Word is always His will. *Always.*

We can resist those deadly distractions with God's help and a fierce determination to stay on His path.

Eve rationalized her decision to eat the forbidden fruit. She saw that it was pleasing, desirable, and good for food. Distractions never come wrapped as deadly, but delectable and delicious. That's just how cunning and crafty the devil is. He refutes the deadly consequences of distractions and disobedience and entices us with delicacies from the Devil's Diner. All the dishes are made to order, always delicious, but deadly, laced with his slow-killing poison. They will destroy your life, sooner or later. What if chocolate cake was your favorite dessert and you were offered some by a colleague. It looked great and you were ready to dive in, and then you found out the cake was laced with crystals of cyanide. Would that information change anything? It should. The cake is desirable, but it will kill you with just one slice. Our adversary has one mission: to steal, to kill, and to destroy us, according to John 10:10. Distractions are one of his most effective tools. We often focus on the immediate gratification, not the long-term ramifications. Romans 6:23 says, "The wages of sin is death, but the gift of God is eternal life."

We've learned from the best (Eve), so we rationalize our decision to sin. I want you to pause and ask yourself, "What are my enticing delicacies or distractions? What dish does Satan offer me that I usually accept, but it's destroying me, hindering me from being distinctive for God's purposes?" Study that list so you will recognize the distraction when it comes calling your name.

We can resist those deadly distractions with God's help and a fierce determination to stay on His path. Remember Jesus. He allowed nothing to keep Him from His God-given assignment: the cross, followed by the resurrection, and then redemption from sin for us all.

becoming distinctly
you

1. What distracts you, easily gets you off course? What are your enticing delicacies? Make a list.
2. Name a time when a distraction derailed you from God's best path.

3. What lessons can you apply from the distractions that King David and Adam and Eve succumbed to?

4. What are the deadly consequences of distractions that appear as delicacies and delights?

5. What "dish" does Satan offer you, and you usually accept, that is hindering your distinctiveness for God's purposes?

6. What's your strategy for resisting these distractions in the future?

8

Disappointment With God

Expectations will get you in trouble every time. You expect God to answer your prayers one way and He doesn't. You expect Him to answer within your time frame. It passes. You dream big dreams of what you want to accomplish for God and His glory, and they never materialize. You hold on to all the faith Scriptures, posting them on cards all over the house. Still nothing. The twin D's, disappointment and depression, descend upon you, blocking your progress to pursue God's desired end for you. You want to run away and hide, but you can't. You have bills to pay and at least one mouth to feed. A good cry will just have to do.

We all dream big dreams for our lives, careers, and families. Many times, those dreams are what propelled us to choose a particular college, major, job, mate, and neighborhood. We know the success stories of famous people like Bill Gates, Venus and Serena Williams, Dr. Ben Carson, Mark Zuckerberg, and Taylor Swift.

We sometimes wonder if our dreams and desires are realistic, especially if they are not materializing. We wonder whether they are the right dreams and how we can make them happen. We are *still* not married. We're in a dead-end, unstimulating profession, childless, or married with children and depressed.

When I'm disappointed, I can usually trace it to an expectation not being met. If you're single, you probably know how it works. You meet someone and start texting, emailing, or having phone conversations. You develop a regular rhythm of communicating. Then the person stops cold. You don't know why. You didn't discuss it, but you assumed you would be in touch every week. You're afraid to think what the silence could mean. So you have a meltdown, regretting that you got your hopes up. Maybe you progress to dating and you enjoy the time together. Things are going so smoothly. You expect the relationship to go somewhere. For women, that somewhere is preferably to the altar. When we get signals it is not heading in that direction, we experience frustration, dismay, a sense of rejection, and anger. Chances are the guy never thought beyond the dates, but just enjoyed them. He was just having a good time in the moment. We were running warp speed ahead, already dreaming of wedding dresses and bridesmaids. I've done this so many times: running ahead of God, and the man. It's comical now.

We can be so consumed with our fantasies and desires that our expectations can prevent us from receiving God's best. Jeremiah 29:11 says, "'For I know the plans I have for you,' declares the Lord, 'plans to prosper you and not to harm you, plans to give you hope and a future.'"

Our expectations can cause us to leave God out of the equation because we have plans that we like and we have already written the script. But He tells us in Isaiah 55:8–9: "'For my thoughts are not your thoughts, neither are your ways my ways,' declares the Lord. 'As the heavens are higher than the earth, so are my ways higher than your ways and my thoughts than your thoughts.'" Many times we are more consumed with our expectations than with God's plans.

We can be so consumed with our fantasies and desires that our expectations can prevent us from receiving God's best.

That's how I was when I went for a job interview with a national cable news network. The round of interviews went extremely well (so I thought). I was hoping for a major career move. Before arriving I had already decided that I would not mention to the bureau chief that I had worked on two different shows with an executive now on his staff. I also elected not to call the woman in advance to let her know about the job interview. I had done a great job as her producer in these two different assignments, but I was reluctant to tell her about the interview. My gut told me that if she knew, she would try to sabotage it.

I was near the end of my visit, and things were going very well. The interviewer said he'd be in touch soon. There were others on his team he wanted me to meet. It sounded promising. I was already dreaming of a call in a day or so with a job offer. Then the executive popped her head into the bureau chief's office. He introduced us and she indicated we were "good friends." I would not call us "friends." My heart sank. I didn't want her to have any part of the decision-making. I thought, *Why did she have to show up?*

The former colleague called me that evening at home, something she had never done. She asked tons of questions about the interview and hung up. I never got a follow-up call or letter from the bureau chief. I was so disappointed and upset. I had no proof, but my fingers pointed to my former colleague. All was going well until she arrived on the scene. What did she say or do? I will never know. I eventually realized that I had to let my disappointment go and remember that God is sovereign. I told myself that if the network was going to offer me a job, but God didn't want me to have it, then He used her to block it. No one can stop God from being God. "For all things serve you" (Psalm 119:91).

I heard a pastor say once, "When God doesn't do the lesser, He does the greater." That's what He did in raising Lazarus from the dead. His sisters, Mary and Martha, expected their close friend Jesus to come immediately when they sent this message: "Lord, the one you love is sick" (John 11:3). They knew Jesus to be their close friend and a healer. But verse 6 says, "So when he heard that Lazarus was sick, he stayed where he was two more days." Jesus stayed put. He did not rush to Lazarus's bedside. His sisters were puzzled and baffled by this.

When Jesus did arrive, Lazarus had been in the tomb for four days. Mary and Martha had the same response when they saw Him in verses 21 and 32: "If you had been here, my brother would not have died." So they not only expected Jesus to drop everything and come, but they also expected Him to heal Lazarus and prevent him from dying. Jesus had other plans. He always does. It's always grander than what we could imagine. "Jesus called in a loud voice, 'Lazarus, come out!' The dead man came out" (John 11:43–44).

Disappointments and delays are always for a reason from God's perspective. Unless you believe this in every area of your life, you will be full of resentment, anger, and bitterness. You will miss your distinction and how God wants to write your unique story. Beware of putting God in a box. Beware of your own timetable. He always knows what He's going to do to bring about His purposes in your life.

becoming distinctly you

1. Name a time when you were disappointed with God. How did you express it?
2. What role did your expectations play in the disappointment?
3. Have you ever been more consumed with your expectations than with God's plans for your life? If so, make a list of those expectations.
4. Was there ever a time when your disappointment with God was actually a blessing in disguise?

—— Nugget ——

Practice thanking God when life does not work according to your expectations. Write a list of things that haven't gone as expected. Review it regularly. Offer praise for God's sovereignty and wisdom.

9

Destructive Speech

I have been a talker for as long as I can remember. I have six older brothers, and once when we went to the public health clinic to get our immunization shots for school, I couldn't wait for my mother to pick us up to give her the report. As soon as I got in the car I said, "Mom, Darrell cried and Jerry cried, but I didn't cry!" My brothers would often say, "You tell Momma everything! You're nothing but a reporter, a tattletale!" At the time, I considered that a compliment. I went on to get paid for my reporting.

Over the years I've learned that every day I pack a powerful weapon, a little instrument inside my mouth, the tongue, which only gets sharper with use. If we are not careful, it can become a critical, catty, conniving, and callous instrument. It can slice and dice someone's reputation and good standing in less than a minute. It can destroy a lifelong relationship in seconds. It can block the sweet aroma of distinctiveness we were designed to emit.

We live in a culture that says, "If you know it, share it." No matter what it is, if it's the truth, tell it. If you want to blast it, blog it. If you think it, tweet it. If you want to share it (whatever "it" is), put it on Facebook. No information is sacred. People get a thrill out of exposing the good, the bad, and the ugly in a matter of seconds. No time for fact-checking or asking, "Is it wise to do this?" This quick-to-the-draw philosophy is not in step with God's timeless truths about our tongue. "Too much talk leads to sin" (Proverbs 10:19 NLT).

I've discovered the longer I talk, the greater my chances of saying something I should not say and sinning with my tongue. I'm just talking to be talking. Have you ever had that experience? Your conversation starts out with need-to-know information, and as it progresses you start speculating about other people, questioning and indicting their decisions that have absolutely nothing to do with you. Their situation bombards your mind all day. You can't function at your optimum. You're not praying for them, just thinking about it or telling others about it. Chances are you slipped into the sins of gossip and slander.

What is gossip? It is idle talk or rumor, especially about the personal or private affairs of others. It is habit forming. You can do it without realizing it. It comes so naturally, since "inquiring minds want to know." Gossip is an acceptable cultural pastime because we are inundated with information about the private affairs of those we know and don't know personally as a result of reality TV, celebrity magazines, and all forms of social media. When it doesn't come to us, we can go to it and quell our curiosity.

Gossip is inviting and "delicious." "The words of a gossip are like choice morsels; they go down to the inmost parts" (Proverbs 26:22). I was surprised to find gossip and backstabbing listed in Romans 1 along with murder, envy, and quarreling, and described as the behavior of those who refuse to acknowledge God. He abandoned them to their evil minds and let them do things that should never be done. "Their lives became full of every kind of wickedness, sin, greed, hate, envy, murder, quarreling, deception, malicious behavior, and gossip. They are backstabbers, haters of God, insolent, proud, and boastful" (Romans 1:29–30 NLT).

Where gossip is, slander usually follows. Slander is a malicious, false, and defamatory statement or report. It's spreading false information or rumors with the intent to ruin someone's reputation. It's premeditated. You know exactly what sharing that information will do: It will put a blight on someone's character and ignite a firestorm. Engaging in both of these pastimes is sin. It is so easy for us to be repelled by what we consider the big sins and look with contempt on those who murder or commit adultery. We are smug in our righteousness because we don't do those things—but our words and word count equally matter to God. "And I tell you this, you must give an account on judgment day for every idle word you speak. The words you say will either acquit you or condemn you" (Matthew 12:36–37 NLT).

What a sobering reality that every careless, idle word we speak will be judged by God himself. This is definitely an incentive to only speak when we have something constructive to say. What grade would you give your daily speech? The talk about yourself, and about others.

We can be guilty of tearing ourselves down more than anybody else. We do that with our internal dialogue, our self-talk.

We say things like "I am so clumsy." "I am not pretty." "I don't have much talent." "I'm not college material." "I could never do that." "No one will be interested in me." "At my age, I'll never get married." "I am so disorganized and undisciplined." "I'm too old." "I'll never get ahead."

Motivational speaker Zig Ziglar said the most important conversation we have every day is the one between our two ears. Are you saying to yourself only what God says about you? That is truth. Truth is not what you think or what others think or say about you. Authentic truth is always what God says. Jesus said we must feed on every word of God (see Matthew 4:4).

In order to be distinctive, we must make the choice and develop the habit of rejecting destructive speech about ourselves and instead reflect on the promises of God. We live in a society that focuses on what each person brings to the table. This is what qualifies him or her for the top spot. God says, "That's not how my kingdom works. I choose whom I will. They may not be qualified by the world's standards, but I do the equipping."

So stop the negative talk about you and others. Just as God has made you distinct, so others are distinct. Respect that God knew what He was doing when He crafted the differences of race, personality, intelligence, looks, ability, interests, experiences, and perspective. "Why do you judge your brother? Or why do you show contempt for your brother? For we shall all stand before the judgment seat of Christ. . . . So then each of us will give account of himself to God. Therefore let us not judge one another anymore" (Romans 14:10, 12–13 NKJV).

Miriam got in trouble big-time for criticizing her younger brother Moses. She and her brother Aaron began to talk against Moses because his wife was not Jewish but Ethiopian. That was not the only issue. Stirring under the surface were jealousy, envy, and pride. "Has the Lord spoken only through Moses?" they asked. "Hasn't he also spoken through us?" (Numbers 12:2). They were saying, "God has gifted us as well. We bring something to the table. Why is he the only spokesperson for God?" *Watch out.* There is usually a foul spirit behind our destructive speech about others. What we say can be fueled by jealousy, envy, pride, or a sense of entitlement. Miriam and Aaron held the key powerful positions of priest and prophet, but they resented that Moses (their younger brother) was the leader. Perhaps they thought, *We're older. We didn't murder someone like he did, and we certainly didn't run away for forty years in the desert. We have faithfully followed God all of our lives. Why is he the chosen one?*

Does this internal dialogue sound familiar? You may not have articulated it, but maybe you resent someone else's success, looks, connections, or creativity. You don't like that God has blessed her to see her dreams fulfilled, when you are still struggling financially with your boatload of dreams. You've been faithful to God all of your life; she just got saved yesterday, and one door after another is opening for her. You say, "It's not fair!" So when someone praises her, you chime in with a criticism. You only see your failure when you see her success. You see your inadequacy when you see her accomplishments.

It is critical to immediately deal with the root of our destructive speech about others. When you review your reactions (verbal and nonverbal), be brutally honest about your motives. What was actually behind the cutting remarks? Examine yourself. I do this regularly. I seldom like what comes up. I remember a conversation I had with a peer about a project. During the discussion I mentioned information I had "uncovered" that my predecessor overlooked. Afterward, I was convicted about how

I'd shared my findings. I asked myself, "Why did I feel the need (in a subtle way) to put a colleague down? Was this a way of lifting myself up in the eyes of my peer?" If so, I dishonored God. I never have to put anyone down to elevate myself. My findings were not wrong, but when my heart is pure and loving, I will seek to share the information so as not to defame someone else's character. I won't take joy in uncovering others' missteps. "Above all, love each other deeply, because love covers over a multitude of sins" (1 Peter 4:8).

God is always checking out the spirit behind what we do and what we say. It may be the truth, but if it is not shared in love, with the right motive, with the right tone, and at the right time, God will be displeased. When I searched my heart, I realized that I did have a problem with this woman. I did not like her attitude. I found her difficult. I immediately asked God to forgive me and to place within my heart a genuine love for her as she was, not for how I wanted her to be.

Again, it's not wrong to point out missteps or information that (if left alone) could be detrimental to the company or individual, but we must always check our spirit and motive for doing so to make sure there is no hidden agenda to raise our profile while lowering someone else's. We need to uncover what is fueling the revelation. Is it resentment, jealousy, anger, disgust, or pride? Remember, God is always listening to our internal and external dialogue.

After Miriam said, "Hasn't he also spoken through us?" the next sentence is "And the Lord heard this" (Numbers 12:2). God's displeasure came swiftly. He appeared in a cloud and summoned Aaron and Miriam. When both stepped forward, he said that Moses was His faithful servant and that He spoke to him face-to-face. "Why then were you not afraid to speak against my servant Moses?" (Numbers 12:8). When God stopped speaking and the cloud lifted above the tent, Miriam had leprosy; her skin was like snow. In shock, Aaron pleaded with Moses for forgiveness and healing for Miriam. Moses then cried out to God on her behalf. God heard his prayer, but with one caveat: Miriam was to be confined outside the camp for seven days. Upon her return, she was cured of leprosy.

God is always listening to our internal and external dialogue.

Aren't you glad that God in His mercy has not inflicted us with leprosy or another disease because of the sins of the tongue? He takes our speech seriously; let us do the same and monitor it before it leaves our mouth. Search what's behind the thought before it's spoken. It could be blocking your distinctiveness or opportunities.

I have learned that because I am not hesitant to communicate my thoughts, I have to be extremely careful and prayerful. I used to get them out immediately (let it rip), and then, of course, regret what I said, how I said it, and when. Now I find it more effective to wait, calm down, and pray about what I'm going to say, how I'm going to say it, and when. I'm more sensitive to speaking the truth in love without offending the person or allowing my ego to get in the mix. When I consistently do this, asking God to guide my thoughts and my tongue, my speech is much more effective, and God is glorified in the process. I am still a work in progress, aiming for an A+. Whenever I am prompted and tempted to let them know exactly what I think . . . *now*, I know this is usually not God. It's self or Satan attempting to trip me up to speak destructive words that will cut deeply or undermine a relationship. "Gracious words promote instruction" (Proverbs 16:21). Let's be distinctive with words that build up, not blast; encourage, not indict; correct, not condemn.

becoming distinctly
you

1. What grade do you give your daily speech, the way you talk about yourself and others?

2. What is the ongoing dialogue you have between your ears?

3. Authentic truth is always what God says, not what you think. How often do you reflect on this principle and live by it?

4. Review some of the destructive comments you've made recently (verbal or nonverbal). Be brutally honest with yourself. What were the motives behind the cutting remarks, the stinging criticism?

5. Matthew 12:34 says, "Out of the abundance of the heart the mouth speaks" (NKJV). Consider the importance of checking your spirit and mouth before sharing hurtful information. How may this influence what you say?

6. What steps do you take to monitor your words before they leave your mouth?

——— *Nugget Prayer* ———

Lord, I need help with my destructive speech. If left to myself, I am prone to say exactly what I think, in the wrong tone, at the wrong time, causing more harm than good. Lord, forgive me. I only want to use this powerful, sharp instrument to build up, not tear down. I promise to examine my heart before I speak to ensure that my motives are right before proceeding. Remove all pride from me. Every ounce. I know that you hate pride. May I speak only as an act of love, and model the Proverbs 31 woman. May kindness be the rule for everything I say (Proverbs 31:26).

10

A Bad Attitude

Do you know someone with a bad attitude, always negative and critical? You know that when you say "Good morning" and "How are you?" you are going to get an earful of what's going wrong in their world. You brace yourself because you know the avalanche is coming. God never wants our distinctiveness or what sets us apart from the pack to be a bad attitude. It stinks in His nostrils and to those around us.

Negativity is a habit. If exercised every day, it becomes a natural response that operates on autopilot. I've observed this while engaging in small talk with some people. If it's winter, they say, "Oh, it's so cold outside. Unbearable." I say in return, "Well, I'm thankful that I don't live in Boston, where they are experiencing record snowfall." They say in return, "Oh yeah, that's right. It's not as bad here." When it's summer they say, "Oh, it is so hot. Steamy." I say, "I am so thankful that I have air conditioning in my car and my home." Most of the time we don't recognize that we are complaining about the simple things of life that we have no control over, like the weather.

Our poor attitude may result from some unresolved issues in our lives: childhood hurts, job loss, loneliness, marital breakup, prolonged illness, and festering anger. The prophet Jonah personified a bad attitude. It's on display when God tells him to take the gospel to one of Israel's most dreaded enemies, the people of Assyria. "The word of the Lord came to Jonah son of Amittai: 'Go to the great city of Nineveh and preach against it, because its wickedness has come up before me'" (Jonah 1:1–2).

God gave His prophet a direct, easy to understand assignment: Go to Nineveh and speak on my behalf. What did Jonah do? He ran the other direction to another town. God told him to go east. He went west. He didn't want to do what God called him to do. Nineveh was a wicked city inhabited by non-Jews. This was not Jonah's dream job. He'd rather go AWOL than offer the Assyrians a chance to hear the gospel and repent. Disobedience (even in small matters) is always a sign of a bad attitude and poor judgment. Jonah found this out the hard way when God provided a great fish to swallow him alive when he was thrown into the sea.

Why do we think life will go well for us when we are out of God's perfect will and defiant? What do we expect to gain or how can we possibly enhance our lives when we're holding on to that rebellion year after year? It's only blocking God's distinct path. It's not a path of anger, resentment,

Disobedience (even in small matters) is always a sign of a bad attitude and poor judgment.

85

and bitterness. It's a path of wholeness, abundant living, and peace when we choose to obey and walk in it.

It's helpful to assess the cause of our negativity, but we shouldn't stay parked there. Ask the hard questions: "Why am I resentful? Why did I respond rudely? Why do I intentionally avoid that person? Why did I roll my eyes at that woman?" Once you have your answers, ask, "How would Christ want me to respond?" I say that because so many times we think our attitudes are justifiable because of the pain or betrayal we've experienced, and that God will understand.

I remember the intense heartbreak when my husband walked out of our marriage after only three years. I couldn't believe this was happening to me. I loved God with all my heart. Surely He would intervene and bring about a reconciliation. He had the power to do so. But He did not.

One day I sat on my bed and opened my Bible. My eyes wandered to Luke 6:27–28: "But to you who are listening I say: Love your enemies, do good to those who hate you, bless those who curse you, pray for those who mistreat you." I read it again to make sure I was reading correctly. Of course I had read this Scripture many times in my life, but then I wasn't experiencing heartbreak. Now it seemed a little extreme given my situation. I focused again on the only options given: love, do good, bless, and pray for my enemies. The tears began to flow. I didn't want to do that. I said, "Lord, I know how to read, so I can't act like I don't know what you're asking of me. Your instructions are clear. I don't want to do this, but I am going to obey you."

As soon as my will lined up with the will of God and I confessed my allegiance to Him, a change took place in my heart. God stepped in and gave me the strength to do what I could not do in my own strength. It was amazing. My heart began to soften. Resentment began to dissipate.

I'm not saying that my emotional healing was complete at that moment, but when we decide in advance to release any attitudes that are displeasing to God, He will step in and help us. I can say that from that day forward, I never again experienced deep anger and resentment. On a regular basis I would say, "I choose to love, do good, bless him, and pray for him." The rest of the story is up to God, but I made a deliberate decision to *refuse* to be an angry woman, filled with bitterness and resentment, and down on the institution of marriage.

Sometimes we can obey God and our attitude still stinks. That's what happened to our friend Jonah. God gave him a second chance after he prayed to the Lord while being inside the great fish for three days and nights. Nineveh didn't look so bad after all from that perspective. "Then the word of the Lord came to Jonah a second time: 'Go to the great city of Nineveh and proclaim to it the message I give you.' Jonah obeyed the word of the Lord and went to Nineveh" (Jonah 3:1–3). He preached a powerful, God-given message of destruction for the city. The people, including the king, repented. God saw their sincerity and acted with compassion and decided not to carry out His threat of destruction.

God's mercy angered Jonah. He wanted them destroyed. They deserved it. They were a Gentile nation. Have you ever been upset that God showed kindness to one of your enemies? In your opinion, God was letting them off the hook with a good life. Maybe circumstances appear to be easier for them than for you. The woman who was once an adulterer is in a happy marriage, with children, living the "good" life; you accepted

Christ as a child and were faithful in your marriage, but now you're struggling as a single parent, trying to make ends meet.

God loves everybody and is no respecter of persons (John 3:16; 1 John 4:10; Acts 10:34). He rains on the just as well as the unjust (Matthew 5:45). He does whatever He wills (Psalm 115:3). Who are we to dictate to God whom He blesses and curses (Exodus 33:19)? Jonah was so disgusted by God's kindness to the city of Nineveh that he wanted to die. "Now, Lord, take away my life, for it is better for me to die than to live" (Jonah 4:3). Was Jonah embarrassed that his dire predictions did not come true? Did he value his reputation more than God's reputation? God said to Jonah, "Is it right for you to be angry?" (Jonah 4:4). God didn't think so. Jonah was being self-centered. God was looking at the bigger picture of sparing a city of 120,000 people because they humbled themselves and repented.

Examine your heart when you're negative. Refuse to let it define you. Ask God to help you process pain, despair, anger, and resentment from His perspective. Good will come from it. As painful as my marital episode was, I sensed God's presence with me every step of the way. He did not reject me during my negativity and "woe is me" days. He was tender and compassionate and allowed me to vent. The Lord spoke to me one day and said, "Cheryl, it's time for you to take a long, hard look at yourself. No one else. There are some things I want to teach you during this ordeal. I need you to focus on that. In your prayers, ask me what it is I want you to learn. Otherwise, you won't learn the lessons." After that, I changed my focus and my attitude. I humbled myself and sincerely wanted God to teach me, to show me *me*. I experienced spiritual brokenness. He was ready to go to work.

becoming distinctly you

1. Name some bad attitudes you detect in yourself.

2. Can you identify with Jonah? Name a time God's Word clearly spelled out one course of action and you did the opposite. Why did you do it? What was the outcome?

3. Ask yourself these hard questions:

   Why am I resentful of _____?

   Why did I respond rudely when _____?

   Why do I intentionally avoid _____?

4. A bad attitude is a choice. So is an excellent attitude. What bad attitudes do you need to release?

5. Be honest. Have you ever been upset that God showed kindness to one of your enemies? If so, why?

~ Nugget ~

Pray now and ask God to heal your resentment and bitterness and disappointment. Ask for forgiveness for your disobedience.

11

Spiritual Apathy

Apathy about God stalls our distinction. On this journey I've learned that our relationship with God must be nurtured in order to thrive. It's easy for apathy to set in when we allow other relationships or pursuits to dominate our thinking and our time. Today, are you consumed with God and His will for your life? Are you passionate about serving Him? Does it bring you great joy? Or are you simply going through the motions of church attendance, praying, and reading your Bible? Perhaps the thrill, quite honestly, is gone. These items are simply on your check-off list to be a good Christian. *Beware.* As Chuck Swindoll says, "Erosion . . . is always silent; it is always slow; it is always subtle. But its final blow is always severe."[1]

If we're not careful, life happens, and God is no longer number one in our lives. We don't mean for it to happen, but other things and people take priority and God is pushed out of His prominent spot at the top. We stop cultivating intimacy with Him. We just stop talking to Him as much as we did early on in the relationship. We get busy with our agenda, commitments, and responsibilities. A routine sets in.

This phenomenon is not new. Jesus was asked what the greatest commandment is. He answered, "Love the Lord your God with all your heart and with all your soul and with all your mind and with all your strength" (Mark 12:30). All means *all*, with every fiber of our being. This is an all-consuming love. This same commandment is mentioned several times in the Old Testament. In the last book of the Bible, Revelation, in chapter 2, this was the message

Are you consumed with God and His will for your life?

to the church in Ephesus. It had a reputation for good deeds, hard work, and perseverance. It did not tolerate sin among its members, but God had a major problem with this church that on the surface was performing well and looked great and prosperous. Christ said in Revelation 2:4, "Yet I hold this against you: You have forsaken the love you had at first." Your first love. You are busy doing great things, but you are not building a relationship of authentic love. Your actions are not motivated by a heart of love. You are more enthralled by the mission and the ministry than your Master.

Paul praised this church in its early years. In Ephesians 1:15–16 he said, "For this reason, ever since I heard about your faith in the Lord Jesus and your love for all God's people, I have not stopped giving thanks for you, remembering you in my prayers." The Ephesian church was once known for its faith and love, but not anymore. Now it was known for actions and programs, devoid of a fervent love for God and the saints. God noticed the distance and held it against them.

What are the signs that we no longer have freshness in our relationship with God? That our love for Him is no longer vibrant and first place in our lives? Here are some:

- It's not a priority to give Him our best time when we are alert and focused. We are snatching minutes here and there on the run.
- We sporadically read the Bible. It's "hit and miss," many times just "miss."
- We are engaged in Christian activities out of duty, social correctness, expectations, and payoff rather than because they please God and are acts of kindness and love.
- We spend more time with God when we want or need something. We desire His gifts more than Him.
- In church we are simply going through the motions of worship and hearing the Word. We are there in body but not in spirit. Our minds are distracted.
- We see quiet time and devotions as more of an obligation than a joy.

We are to do three things to rectify this apathy: remember, repent, and return. Remember how it used to be. Think about your first love and how it was when you fell in love. You felt good all over. You could not get him out of your mind. Every chance you got, you talked about him. You treasured every conversation. When you weren't together, just thinking about him brought a smile to your face. You looked forward to every phone call, every date. It didn't matter where, it just mattered that you were together. You savored his love letters and read them often. You didn't want to leave his presence. You sang the song "If Loving You Is Wrong, I Don't Want to Be Right."

God desires that same kind of intimacy. He wants us to long to be with Him. He wants us to love reading His love letter to us, the Bible, regularly, and to love meditating on His words throughout the day, as often as we can. He wants us to live for Him and Him alone. He desires that we want to do what pleases Him, not out of fear, but out of love. He desires our relationship with Him to be the most important relationship in our lives and that we find absolute delight in Him with no strings attached.

It's easy for women to understand this concept because we long for a man to love us for who we are and for no other reason. We want no competition with any other woman. God understands a spouse's jealousy because of a mate's divided heart. He's been there and He hates it.

The greatest challenge for Christians since the beginning of time has been cultivating an undivided heart. The first of the Ten Commandments is "You shall have no other gods before me" (Exodus 20:3). That's another way of saying, "Don't love anything or anyone more than me."

Despite all the miracles the children of Israel witnessed when God delivered them from Egypt, he tells them repeatedly, "Love the Lord your God with all your heart and with all your soul and with all your strength" (Deuteronomy 6:5). In chapter 10, verse 12, God says, "And now, Israel, what does the Lord your God ask of you but to fear the Lord your God, to walk in obedience to him, to love him, to serve the Lord your God with all your heart and with all your soul."

David was not perfect, but he was known as a man after God's own heart (see Acts 13:22). He loved God intensely. Here are examples of the intensity of his love: "One thing I ask from the Lord, this only do I seek: that I may dwell in the house of the Lord all the days of my life" (Psalm 27:4); "How priceless is your unfailing love" (Psalm 36:7); "You, God, are my God, earnestly I seek you; I thirst for you, my whole being longs for you. . . . Your love is better than life. . . . On my bed I remember you; I think of you through the watches of the night. . . . I cling to you" (Psalm 63:1, 3, 6, 8).

Can you relate to what David is saying? He is not ashamed of his all-consuming love for God. His identity and his worth are derived from this relationship. It's the one thing he can't live without. It is priceless. He seeks God, thirsts for God, longs for Him, and thinks of Him constantly. His love relationship with God was his lifeline. It gave him confidence and perspective on navigating life successfully. A vibrant relationship with God is what will fuel your confidence as you walk in your God-ordained purpose.

It was when David grew apathetic in his relationship with God, and his love grew cold and distant, that he fell into sin. He stopped doing what he used to do. We've seen this same phenomenon play out in our relationships. We stop communicating with that friend or spouse. We stop making quality time for each other. Soon there's a shift in the relationship. We are no longer connecting, sharing joys as well as frustrations. Life gets busy. The friendship is crowded out. We look up one day and there is a distance. At that point we have a choice: Make an attempt to rekindle the relationship or let it die.

When the prophet Nathan confronted David about his adultery, the king acknowledged that he had sinned against God and he needed to return to his first love. David was broken and repentant. He penned Psalm 51, and said, "Against you, you only, have I sinned" (v. 4). He cried out for God to create in him a pure heart and renew a steadfast spirit within him (v. 10). He once again longed for intimacy with God.

To cast aside spiritual apathy, remember when Christ first captured your heart, and then, like David, come clean and repent. Give no excuses. Just confess your shortcomings and sins and ask God to forgive you. First John 1:9 says, "If we confess our sins, he is faithful and just and will forgive us our sins and purify us from all unrighteousness." Repentance means we are sincerely sorry for our sins and we are ready to forsake them and make a U-turn back to God. We truly regret that we have grown cold or indifferent regarding the things of God and our love relationship with Him. If we're honest, sometimes we enjoyed the sin and now need a willing spirit to forsake it. Sin can be pleasurable. We know that sex outside of marriage displeases God, but it pleases us. When we're dealing with an enticing sin, it's important to pray for a willing heart and mind to do the right thing and to forsake any thoughts or actions that grieve the heart of God.

Once we have repented, we then return. We return to the things we used to do to keep the relationship vibrant and alive. We make it a priority to spend time daily with God. We read His Word, allowing Him to talk to us. We pray—talking to Him about everything that concerns us. Then we think about Him and His goodness (meditation) as often as we can. He is ever in our thoughts. We seek to so cultivate our love relationship that it defines our choices and our actions. That's the kind of reverence Joseph had for God. He was single, handsome, and well built, the Bible says. When he was propositioned on a regular basis by his boss's wife, Joseph said, "How then could I do such a wicked thing and sin against God?" (Genesis 39:9).

His decision did not take into account his libido or testosterone as a virile young man. His love for God was greater than his passions.

This is always my prayer: that my love for God would be so intense and so all-consuming that I have no desire to think, say, or do anything that would displease God. It should be God's love that constrains us from sinning, not the fear of getting caught or going to hell. Think about it: When we are in a loving, satisfying relationship, we don't want to do anything to hurt our beloved or hamper the friendship. We think twice before we say or do something. We don't want to offend or belittle. We cherish the friendship.

The dividends are priceless when we give Him first place in our lives.

God says good works are not enough for Him. Lip service is not enough. He forever wants our hearts. He always wants to be our first love. The dividends are priceless when we give Him first place in our lives. Are you experiencing spiritual apathy? You can reverse it immediately. Just remember how it used to be between you and God when you first fell in love; repent for falling short; then make a conscious decision to "make up" and return. You won't regret it. He will receive you with open arms without condemnation. After all, He's been waiting.

becoming distinctly
you

1. Are you consumed with God's will for your life or *your* dreams, desires, and goals?

2. I mentioned six signs of spiritual apathy in this chapter. Which ones do you most identify with?

3. Has there been slippage over time? What caused it?

4. Review the steps for restoration: remember, repent, and return. What can you do to nourish your relationship with God to ensure it is your number-one priority?

5. What actions or activities do you need to resume (putting God in the number-one slot) to refuel your relationship?

—— *Nugget* ——

Decide today to repent like David did and acknowledge moving God out of first place. Be honest about your sins and shortcomings. Ask God for a willing heart and mind to reject sin and for the grace to do the right thing.

Lord, thank you for cherishing me and always desiring relationship with me. I'm sorry I moved away from intimate fellowship with you. By your grace, I forsake all thoughts and actions that grieved your heart. Please forgive me. I want to be all yours to accomplish your purposes as a distinct vessel. Wash and cleanse me. Restore the joy of my salvation. May my love for you be intense and all-consuming so that I am guided only by your love. Thank you in advance.

12

Seeing Failure as Final

Everybody has failed at something. No one is perfect, so why do we try to act like we are or spend countless hours attempting to hide our failures and imperfections? Women specialize in this. We have an arsenal of undergarments and beauty products that promise to correct or rearrange our flaws and defy the aging process. But focusing on our external appearance does not address the internal dialogue of being a failure in life.

It's important to remember that failing and being a failure are two different things. All have failed because all have sinned, missed the mark of God's best life. That's why we needed a perfect sacrifice, Jesus Christ, to take away all of our sins by his death on the cross.

Billionaire investor Warren Buffett says, "There is no question that you are going to make mistakes in life. I've made a lot, and I'm going to make more. You just have to make sure that your blunders are never fatal. . . . You have to put your mistakes behind you and not look back."[1]

It is so easy for us to throw up our hands in surrender and give up on ourselves and life when we make a horrible decision. We think, "I've blown it big time now. My chances are shot at living a life of distinction, and being all that God called me to be." *Wrong.* When I was going through the greatest crisis of my life, initially I confused a failed marriage with being a failure. I felt like there was a big *D* on my forehead that meant "failure, failure, failure." All my life my goal was to be the perfect Christian, pleasing God in every way. I wanted no heartache, no pain, no mistakes, just a track record of always making the right choice in every situation. Who do you know, except God, who has *always* made the right decision about everything? I was setting myself up for failure trying to live out this goal.

I got a different perspective one Sunday morning when I heard a message from Dr. Charles Stanley on Peter's three-time denial of his precious Lord. First, Peter never saw himself as capable of failing the Lord. What encouraged me is the reminder of what Jesus told Peter in advance of his fall: "Simon, Simon, Satan has asked to sift all of you as wheat. But I have prayed for you, Simon, that your faith may not fail. And when you have turned back, strengthen your brothers" (Luke 22:31–32). Dr. Stanley pointed out that Peter's failure did not catch God by surprise. In advance of the fall, Jesus didn't pray that Peter would not fail, but that his faith would not fail. This revelation changed my perspective. When I examined my ordeal, the reality was that our marriage had failed, but my faith in God was intact and stronger than ever. It was my faith in God and His sovereignty that allowed me to get through each day. Not only did Jesus pray for Peter's faith, but He also affirmed that He still had a great destiny for Peter, and once Peter reaffirmed his commitment to Christ, he was charged with strengthening others. Peter's failure did not cancel his God-given assignment.

Now, what if after denying Jesus three times, Peter could not forgive himself, or ask God for forgiveness, and instead chose to wallow in self-pity, constantly rewinding the tape of his betrayal? What if his attitude had been, "I cannot show my face around the other disciples ever again. I might as well resign from the group, because God will never use me again, not after what I did. I will never get over my betrayal. I am a despicable man." Instead, Peter accepted God's marvelous grace. When He forgives us, He remembers our sins no more. They are cast into the sea of forgetfulness.

When Peter heard the news of Jesus' resurrection, he got up and ran to the tomb. "Bending over, he saw the strips of linen lying by themselves, and he went away, wondering to himself what had happened" (Luke 24:12).

Later, when Jesus appeared to the disciples while fishing, and John announced that it was Jesus standing on the shore, Peter was the first discile to jump in the water and swim toward Jesus. When you fail horribly, do you run away from God or run to God? Judas chose to run away from God, ending his life in suicide. Peter chose to run to the Savior. Jesus never once condemned Peter. He asked him a series of questions in John 21. Three times Jesus wanted to know if Peter really loved him. Each time, Peter answered yes. In response, Jesus said, "I have work for you to do. I want you to feed my sheep (my followers)" (see vv. 15–17).

Peter went on to be one of the great apostles and leaders in the church. On the day of Pentecost, after he was filled with the Holy Spirit, Peter stood up and boldly addressed the crowd with the gospel message. They asked Peter what the next step was. He responded, "Repent, and be baptized every one of you in the name of Jesus Christ for the remission of sins, and ye shall receive the gift of the Holy Ghost. For the promise is unto you, and to your children, and to all that are afar off, even as many as the Lord our God shall call" (Acts 2:38–39 KJV). After Peter's stirring message, about three thousand people became converts to Christianity. What a stirring example of failure not being final!

When you fail horribly, do you run away from God or run to God?

When you fail, you have a choice: Wallow in it and beat yourself up forever and always, or learn from the mistakes, be a better person, and walk in God's mercy and grace, accepting any potential consequences. That's what David did after he committed adultery with Bathsheba. God forgave him, but there would be consequences: The baby would die, and one of his own sons would commit adultery with David's wives in public, in broad daylight (see 2 Samuel 12:11, 17). God did not change His mind about the punishment, despite pleas from David.

No matter how low or how public the fall, the disgrace, God is not shocked. He still has great plans for your destiny. His blueprint included the failure. He's already made provisions to re-route you. Don't get stuck on failure. Take on the attitude that the apostle Paul lived by: "I have not achieved it, but I focus on this one thing: Forgetting the past and looking forward to what lies ahead, I press on to reach the end of the race and receive the heavenly prize for which God, through Christ Jesus, is calling us" (Philippians 3:13–14 NLT). He too could have rehearsed his failure of zealously persecuting Christians and being responsible for many deaths. Paul made a deliberate decision to put his past behind him and concentrate on the goal in front of him, receiving a commendation from God.

It's okay to glance in the rearview mirror, but if you decide to gaze, an accident is imminent. Keep your eyes on the prize in front of you. It's attainable.

becoming distinctly you

1. Name a failure for which you find it difficult to forgive yourself.

2. When you fail horribly, do you run *away* from God or run *to* God? What are the dangers of running away from God? What are the benefits of running to God?

3. Reflect on Peter's failure (denying Jesus) and restoration. What are the lessons for you?

4. What are the deliberate choices you need to make to move forward after failure?

Part Two

Distinctly You
Builders

13

Let God Define You

All of creation is content to be what it was made to be, except man. Fish flourish in water. Ants are not depressed about their size; they are productive, building massive colonies. We waste time aiming at the bull's-eye on someone else's board, pursuing a race we were never equipped to run.

Let God, not you or the culture, define you and your distinction. You are His masterpiece. There are more than seven billion people in the world, but no one exactly like you. Nothing about you is a mistake because God doesn't make mistakes. He took extreme care in sculpting you with everything you need for accomplishing His purpose. When God created you, it was with a predetermined course in mind, an assignment just for you. "Everything got started in him and finds its purpose in him" (Colossians 1:17 The Message). Because you are His creation, it's important that God defines you and no one else. You will be tempted to forget this from time to time because so many competing forces want that opportunity: you, your family, friends, co-workers, enemies, and the media. You must resist them all. If you don't, you will never become all God intended you to be. I admit it's easier to adapt to someone else's concept of you, accept that label (even if it's negative), or mimic a friend than to spend quality time developing an intimate relationship with the only One who knows why you are here in the first place. Quality relationships always take work.

Before you were born, God selected your parents, your intellect, your looks, your race, your gifts, and your talents. Your mother may have told you that you were a mistake. Maybe for her, but not for God because He doesn't make mistakes. It doesn't matter the circumstances of your birth, planned or unplanned. God was not caught sleeping that day. You were in His mind before you were born. God told Jeremiah: "Before I formed you in the womb I knew you, before you were born I set you apart; I appointed you as a prophet to the nations" (Jeremiah 1:5). Notice that Jeremiah did not stop God midsentence to tell Him about *his* dreams or visions for his life. He didn't ask God to orchestrate his long-held desires. Jeremiah recognized that the sovereign God of the universe, who created everything, and who knows everything about everything, was speaking. Jeremiah's Creator told him, "I knew you before the sexual act occurred that created you. I set you apart because I have a distinct assignment, an appointment for you."

Those words don't only apply to Jeremiah. Yes, the assignment was specific, to be a prophet at a particular time to a particular people, but the God of Jeremiah is living today and does not change. He has a specific role for you. It may be in your home, on your job, in your neighborhood, or on the world's grand stage. It is uniquely crafted for you. He ordained that you would be alive now to accomplish it. What I love about letting God define us is that what He has in mind is usually more massive and exciting than we could ever imagine. Our race, gender, looks, pedigree, intelligence, natural abilities, and age cannot hold us back when we are in sync with His purpose. There is no greater joy than knowing that you are right where God wants you to be, doing exactly what He had in mind for you.

What God has in mind is usually more massive and exciting than we could ever imagine.

It doesn't mean you'll be famous, wealthy, or never encounter struggles, challenges, and heartache. But you can experience peace and contentment because God is right there guiding you every step of the way. He's the navigator. The apostle Paul said,

> I served the Lord with great humility and with tears and in the midst of severe testing by the plots of my Jewish opponents. . . . And now, compelled by the Spirit, I am going to Jerusalem, not knowing what will happen to me there. I only know that in every city the Holy Spirit warns me that prison and hardships are facing me. However, I consider my life worth nothing to me; my only aim is to finish the race and complete the task the Lord Jesus has given me—the task of testifying to the good news of God's grace.
>
> Acts 20:19, 22–24

Paul let God define him and his life's work. He lived for and was consumed with one thing every day: fulfilling the distinct assignment God gave him. It didn't matter what anybody else was doing or what they thought about how he was living his life. Paul made it very clear: I live for God's approval. My goal is to please Him, not man. It wasn't always this way. The first part of his life he spent living out his passionate commitment to stop the flow of Christianity by any means necessary. He was sincere but wrong and misguided. Once he let God define him and clarify his purpose, Paul was never the same.

A couple of obscure guys in the Old Testament were also content to let God define them and their designated role. They thrived as skilled craftsmen for detailed work in constructing the tabernacle.

> Then the Lord said to Moses, "See, I have chosen Bezalel . . . and I have filled him with the Spirit of God, with wisdom, with understanding, with knowledge and with all kinds of skills—to make artistic designs for work in gold, silver and bronze, to cut and set stones, to work in wood, and to engage in all kinds of crafts. Moreover, I have appointed Oholiab . . . to help him. Also I have given ability to all the skilled workers to make everything I have commanded you."
>
> Exodus 31:1–6

God skilled and called Bezalel and Oholiab and other un-named craftsmen for specific tasks, just as he did Moses. He decided in advance which role each would play. Each was vital for carrying out His mandate. We don't find these workers grumbling because they didn't get an out-front assignment with a big title.

Are you ready and willing to discard your dreams and to-tally surrender to God's blueprint for you? Are you *all in* no matter the cost? God will not accept bits and pieces of our agenda interspersed in His master plan. Why would we want to attempt that anyway when whatever we come up with in no way can rival God's awesome plans? Do you think Moses ever dreamed of putting out his rod and parting the Red Sea? Did Sarah imagine having a baby at age ninety? Was it on Daniel's bucket list to spend a peaceful night in a lions' den, the beasts totally uninterested in having him for dinner? When God writes a script, He writes a script that is unrivaled.

My life has been much more exciting and fulfilling than I ever dreamed of growing up in Fifth Ward. God opened some great doors and has led me down some amazing paths of distinction. I wouldn't trade Him as my navigator for Warren Buffett's billions. He says in Isaiah 48:17, "I am the Lord your God, who teaches you what is *best* for you, who directs you in the way you should go" (emphasis mine). There are executives who pay counselors and life coaches thousands of dollars for sage advice that they cannot guarantee is the best course 100 percent of the time. Yet God offers to every person who willingly follows and obeys Him personal coaching that will always steer you along the best route, guaranteed. He promises that His advice is always right because He cannot lie and He knows everything about everything. Who can match that? No one. Unfortunately, every day, billions of people prefer to go their own way, relying on their own intellect, knowledge, and understanding.

So how do you let God define you? It begins with relationship. God wants you to know Him intimately—His voice, how He thinks, what pleases Him, His plans for you. He also wants your heart. Notice, I didn't say He wants you to be a good person, give more to great causes, and increase your church attendance or volunteer efforts. Those things are all good, but our heart is the seat of our emotions and our desires. Our heart rules us. If you give God your heart, He owns you.

If you have a person's heart, you have captured him. Women understand this. What do most women want? To capture a man's heart—not his head, but his heart; not his wallet, but his heart. A woman understands that if she gets his heart, she gets the whole person.

I encourage you to make an intentional decision to give God your most prized possession: your heart, your will. Let seeking Him and loving Him become your first priority. Respect His power and affirm that His written Word, the Bible, is the final authority in your life. Hold Him in the highest esteem and place no one above Him. Be in awe of Him, because it is amazing that almighty God desires to be in intimate relationship with you.

I regularly reaffirm my love and commitment to Christ and let Him know that by His grace, He will always be my number-one love and occupy the top tier of my heart. I remind myself that no one has ever loved me like God, or ever will, and that He proved His love by sending His only Son to die on the cross for my sins. God paid blood money to rescue me from the clutches of sin and take me off the sin auction block. That's just how much He loves me. If He did all that for me (and it had nothing to do with my performance), then I remind myself that I can gladly follow Him anywhere at anytime because I am secure and confident in His love and His motives for directing me down a particular path. I'm happy to ditch my plans for my life. I rehearse and repeat these facts regularly so I know what I stand for and whose side I'm on. I find this necessary, especially since I can have a strong will and idea of how I'd like my life to go. When you let God define you, it's a daily surrender to His will. In return, He gives you great joy and direction.

Letting God define you means your view of yourself is based on how He sees you, not as others see you, and you accept His design.

> We are the clay, you are the potter; we are all the work of your hand.
>
> Isaiah 64:8

> Woe to those who quarrel with their Maker. . . . Does the clay say to the potter, "What are you making?" . . . Woe to the one who says to a father, "What have you begotten?" or to a mother, "What have you brought to birth?" . . . Concerning things to come, do you question me about my children, or give me orders about the work of my hands? It is I who made the earth and created mankind on it.
>
> Isaiah 45:9–12

Finding these verses and reflecting on them were a turning point for me in accepting my design. For as long as I can remember I had questioned why God made me with my temperament, my height, and my appearance when I preferred another package. No one taught me this, but I constantly measured myself against other girls, and I always fell short. I knew I was smart, but I felt inadequate in the looks department. It was especially painful in junior high and high school because no boys were interested in me, not at church or at school. Outwardly, I carried myself like this was not a concern, but inwardly, it hurt. I talked to no one about this but God. I asked, "God, why? What is it about me that no one finds me attractive? I am never picked. Is this how it will always be?" At times I cried in the privacy of my room. No one understood but God. I saw other girls dating and wished that was me.

I eventually found comfort in God's words that He knew exactly what He was doing when He made me exactly as I was. To argue with God meant that I had the audacity to think that He had made a mistake and that I could have done a better job. How ludicrous. I finally learned to rest in the sovereignty of God and His goodness. I developed a routine of reminding myself that *who* I am and *how* I am is God's idea.

All of His ways are right. I am His creation and equipped for His purpose. I also constantly reminded myself that the person God had for me would find me attractive. After all, why would God have a mate for me who was not attracted to me? That didn't make sense. All I needed was one connection. It didn't occur to me until I was much older that with no suitors, God was actually shielding me from heartache and from wasting time and getting distracted from pursuing my education and career. God never does anything without a purpose. It comes down to trusting that God always knows what He is doing and that anything He denies us is for our good. He's not playing games with us and saying no just to make us unhappy. Jesus said,

> Which of you, if his son asks for bread, will give him a stone? Or if he asks for a fish, will give him a snake? If you, then, though you are evil, know how to give good gifts to your children, how much more will your Father in heaven give good gifts to those who ask him!
>
> Matthew 7:9–11

It's a trust issue. Satan always wants us to think that when God denies us something, He is holding back something that is good for us. He's the master of lies. When we fully trust God and His intentions it's easy to let Him define us. We are content with His purposes and plans. We have thrown away our concept of beauty and worth and we embrace His.

God can only define us if we are willing to do whatever He tells us to do. This means making a conscious decision in advance to obey Him in every area of life. No place is off-limits. Your ears are tuned to Him when it comes to managing your finances, your sexual urges, your career, your marriage, your family, and all your relationships. He must reign supreme in every area of your life. He wants it all. When you are distinct, you allow God's Word to be your standard for living, not popular opinion or popular culture; not what your neighbors or co-workers are doing, or what your favorite television show espouses, but God. It is impossible to experience distinction as God intended by going your own way or following the crowd. God told the children of Israel, "Obey My voice, and I will be your God, and you shall be My people. And walk in all the ways that I have com-

I developed a routine of reminding myself that who I am and how I am is God's idea.

manded you, that it may be well with you" (Jeremiah 7:23 NKJV). It doesn't read, Walk in the ways *you* like or choose the ones that are easiest for you, but "walk in all the ways that I have commanded you." Sometimes, what God is telling us to do doesn't make sense from a natural perspective. Sometimes, it gets us out of our comfort zones. It stretches us. Just ask Esther—Queen Esther, that is. I love her God-story.

While the story of Cinderella is my favorite fairy tale, Esther's story is just as intriguing—and it's true. It's found in one of only two books in the Bible named after a woman. Esther was

Jewish, a minority living in Persia, the dominant kingdom in the Middle East at the time. An orphan, Esther was reared by her older cousin Mordecai, who took her as his own daughter when her parents died. Esther 2:7 tells us she was "very beautiful and lovely" (NLT). This verse in *The Message* says, "The girl had a good figure and a beautiful face." God made Esther beautiful on purpose. She had to be a knockout for His divine plan. When the king decided to hold a beauty contest to find the next queen, a search was made for "beautiful young virgins" (2:2) in every province. Esther was selected as a candidate and took part in an exclusive twelve-month beauty regimen on the king's property, in preparation for the king to make his final selection. Whoever pleased the king would become the next queen.

I'm pretty sure Esther did not have a secret longing to be the queen. She had not been dreaming about occupying this position. The last queen, Vashti, displeased the king by her actions and was never again to enter his presence. God's sovereign hand was in all the details. He had created this opportunity for Esther. She had more going for her than just outward beauty. What made her distinct, a standout among all the other beauties?

Esther respected authority. In Esther 2:10, her cousin Mordecai told her not to reveal her nationality (as a Jew) while she was in the king's palace prepping with the other girls. She complied. She was grown, but she listened and respected Mordecai's wisdom and counsel. This was a sign of her ability to be distinctly discreet. Esther knew when to speak and when to keep silent. It was best not to share this information about her heritage, so she kept this secret before she was selected as the next queen and afterward. It says in Esther 2:20, "But Esther had kept secret her family background and nationality just as Mordecai had told her to do, for she continued to follow

Mordecai's instructions as she had done when he was bringing her up." She was selected as queen, yet Esther respectfully followed Mordecai's mandate. We don't see her balking at the request or pulling rank on her cousin because she was now married to the king and no longer living under Mordecai's roof.

Esther not only listened to her cousin but she was also willing to follow the counsel of experienced staff. She was not a know-it-all. Esther 2:15 says that when it was time for her to go to the king, Esther asked for only what her beauty instructor (the chief eunuch) suggested. She followed his lead. She was not a lone ranger taking the lead. She recognized he was the experienced one in these matters. He knew the king's likes and dislikes. Esther "was admired by everyone who saw her" (Esther 2:15 NLT). Are you open to the advice of those more experienced than you in certain areas? God has placed them in your life to help you get where He wants you to go.

When God places us in positions of influence, it is never about us, but about advancing His kingdom and bringing Him glory in our circumstances. God didn't allow Esther to be queen just because she was beautiful. He had a bigger plan. He always does. He was thinking ahead about the deliverance of the Jews.

When God places us in positions of influence, it is never about us, but about advancing His kingdom.

Haman, Mordecai's archenemy, had convinced the king to destroy all the Jews. When Mordecai got news of the plan, he sent word to Esther, urging her to go into the king's presence to beg for mercy for her people. Esther knew the risk (possible death) of approaching the king uninvited. He had not called for her in thirty days. But Mordecai said, "Who knows if perhaps you were made queen for just such a time as this?" (Esther 4:14 NLT).

Esther, full of courage and conviction, said, "Go, gather together all the Jews who are in Susa, and fast for me. Do not eat or drink for three days, night or day. I and my attendants will fast as you do. When this is done, I will go to the king, even though it is against the law. And if I perish, I perish" (Esther 4:15–16).

Almighty God defined Esther and set her up for this strategic position of influence for His purposes. The assignment was bigger than Esther ever dreamed. It always is. Is God calling you to take a stand for Him in your home, on your job, or in your community? Do you fear God, or man? Esther feared only God. She had to do what pleased God even if it meant the loss of the queen's throne. After all, it was only because of God that she was sitting on the throne in the first place.

God always honors those who honor Him. Esther 5:2 says when the king saw Esther standing in his court, he was pleased with her and held out to her the gold scepter. Esther had prepared externally and internally. She had a strategy. When the king asked her about her request, he said he was willing to give her up to half his kingdom. She began, "If it pleases the king, let the king, together with Haman, come today to a banquet I have prepared for him" (Esther 5:4). After that banquet, the king asked Esther again what she would like. She replied, "If the king regards me with favor and it pleases the king to grant my petition and fulfill my request, let the king and Haman come tomorrow to the banquet I will prepare for them. Then I will answer the king's question" (Esther 5:8).

Look at how gracious Esther's speech was. No demands. She acknowledged the king's position and made it clear that she wanted her request to please him. "Words from the mouth of the wise are gracious" (Ecclesiastes 10:12). We can learn so much from Esther. She was tactful. Her example calls for us to step back and think before we speak. As a friend of mine says, "You can say anything to me, if you say it nicely."

Esther possessed an exacting sense of timing. She knew that Haman was her enemy, yet she exercised great restraint in guarding that information until the proper time. The Lord dealt with me years ago about the importance of timing. It is not always expedient to quickly let people know what you know. It can be difficult to hold it, but it can work against you rather than for you, if the truth is not revealed at the proper time. "There is a proper time and procedure for every matter" (Ecclesiastes 8:6). I believe that one reason for Esther's timing (requesting the king's presence at a second banquet) was that she had to be sure that she had his confidence, that he was eating out of her hand first, before she exposed his trusted friend's wicked plot against her and her people.

When the king asked Esther again what she wanted and told her that it would be granted (up to half the kingdom), she was once again tactful and diplomatic: "If I have found favor with you, Your Majesty, and if it pleases you, grant me my life—this is my petition. And spare my people—this is my request" (Esther 7:3). She went on to tell him about the predicament of her people, but once again, she did not point the finger at her enemy, Haman. She had the king eating out of her hand. He asked in a rage, "Who is he? Where is he—the man who has dared to do such a thing?" Esther said, "An adversary and enemy! This vile Haman!" (Esther 7:5–6).

The epic story ends like a fairy tale or a great movie. The bad guy, Haman, gets hanged. The Jews are saved. Esther had such an influence on the king that she was able to give him specifics on how to overturn the edict to kill all the Jews. Once again she was respectful in her tone and with her words. "If it pleases the king," she said, "and if he regards me with favor and thinks it is the right thing to do, and if he is pleased with me, let an order be written overruling the dispatches that Haman . . . devised and wrote to destroy the Jews in all the king's provinces" (Esther 8:5). In her delivery, Esther was not me-centered but king-centered: (1) If it pleases you, (2) if you regard me with favor, (3) if you think it's the right thing to do, and (4) if you are pleased with me. She did not demand; she humbly and graciously asked. It's hard to turn someone down who approaches us in this way. The king did just as Esther suggested.

What influence! Esther let God define her position, one of royalty and wealth. She respected authority and possessed a teachable spirit, as well as courage and conviction. She understood the importance of tact, timing, and diplomacy. One woman, plus her God, saved a nation of people. I call that *distinct*. May we follow Esther's example and greatly influence our generation for the glory of God.

1. List how God defines you.
2. In your own words, what makes *you* distinctly you?

3. Are you all in for God's will to be done in your life, no matter the final outcome? What are the signs that you are willing to do whatever God tells you to do?

4. Letting God define you means your view of yourself is based on how He sees you, not as others see you or you see yourself. You accept His design. Are you there yet? Do you live by this creed? If not, why not?

5. Is God's Word your standard for living? Your final authority? If yes, how do you know? If no, why not?

6. Why are tact, timing, and gracious speech important?

14

Do Your Best

When I was a television reporter in the nation's capital, I did a feature story on Louise, an eighty-three-year-old championship swimmer. I asked her about her goals as a swimmer. Louise had just one. She said in a strong, powerful voice with attitude, "I swim against my *own* number!" That profound statement still rings in my head years later. *I swim against my own number*. Louise was not competing or comparing herself with anyone else. Her goal was to achieve *her* personal best every time she went swimming.

All you can do on the road to distinction is to do *your* best with what you've been given. It doesn't matter what someone else's best is, because chances are your best is not the same. It's not supposed to be. The goal is to make the most of what we have and the least of what we don't have. This means acceptance, fully embracing the person God made you, your particular set of circumstances, and how God wants to use both to chart a distinctive outcome where He gets the glory. There is freedom in striving to do your best and being authentic. You are free of comparing, competing, and coveting.

Doing and being our best always haunts me. It's direct. It's not about anyone else, only our drive, discipline, and determination. When we look at our performance, it's easy to say, "Well, I'm not as gifted as _____," or "Look at that person's credentials, contacts, or cash." But this focus puts the onus squarely on each of us to honestly answer this question: "Am I doing the best with what God has given me?" I believe this is a question we should ask ourselves often. It may cause us to make some much-needed corrections in how we do life.

"Am I doing the best with what God has given me?"

The story of the three servants in Matthew 25 gives us a glimpse into what will take place on judgment day. A man gave his servants money to invest while he was away:

> He gave five bags of silver to one, two bags of silver to another, and one bag of silver to the last—dividing it in proportion to their abilities. He then left on his trip. . . . After a long time their master returned from his trip and called them to give an account of how they had used his money.
>
> vv. 15, 19 NLT

Whatever we have and how much of it we have is determined by God and based on our abilities. What we do with what we have is up to us. His goal is for us to maximize our silver, whether it's one bag or five.

The servant to whom he had entrusted the five bags of silver came forward with five more and said, "Master, you gave me five bags of silver to invest, and I have earned five more." The master was full of praise. "Well done, my good and faithful servant. You have been faithful in handling this small amount, so now I will give you many more responsibilities. Let's celebrate together!"

vv. 20–21

The servant who had been given two bags had the same report: He doubled his amount by investing. He received the identical commendation as the servant who started with five and doubled them.

The master said, "Well done, my good and faithful servant. You have been faithful in handling this small amount, so now I will give you many more responsibilities. Let's celebrate together!"

v. 23

From the owner's perspective, both servants were handling small amounts. They were small in comparison to his abundance. We only have what we've been given. The owner did not demand of the second servant what he did not have, the advantage of starting with three additional bags of silver. His ability level said his capability maximum was two bags to get started. Two would not overwhelm him. He went right to work and maximized his two, doubling them. He didn't waste time wondering why he didn't get five bags of silver like the other servant. There are no signs that he felt insecure because he got less than half of what his colleague received. He wasn't angry about his allotment. The money wasn't his to begin with. When someone gives you a gift, the gracious response is to say thank you, recognizing that you didn't earn it. It was freely given.

124

The third servant faced the owner with a bag of excuses instead of another bag of silver. He blamed his lack of productivity on the owner because he was a "hard man." The worker said he feared losing the money, so he decided the best thing to do was to hide it.

I believe he was unproductive because of jealousy and comparison. He could never get over the fact that he was given only one bag of silver. He felt insignificant, small. *What can I do with just one bag?* he may have thought. He decided to sulk and do nothing. He didn't realize that God was not comparing him with anyone else. He missed the opportunity to win the top commendation in his category.

The owner was livid. He replied,

> "You wicked and lazy servant! If you knew I harvested crops I didn't plant and gathered crops I didn't cultivate, why didn't you deposit my money in the bank? At least I could have gotten some interest on it." Then he ordered, "Take the money from this servant, and give it to the one with the ten bags of silver."
>
> vv. 26–28

The owner accepted no excuses, and neither will God. He knows our capability level. Remember, it was He who doled out the gifts based on our ability. Jesus ends the parable by saying,

> To those who use well what they are given, even more will be given, and they will have an abundance. But from those who do nothing, even what little they have will be taken away.
>
> v. 29

Develop to the fullest what God has given you, whether it's little or much. That's being distinct. We have a wonderful incentive to do our best: We'll be given more. I love how Jean N. Grou puts it:

> Nothing is small or great in God's sight; whatever He wills becomes great to us, however seemingly trifling. Once the voice of conscience tells us that He requires anything of us, we have no right to measure its importance. On the other hand, whatever He would not have us do, however important we may think it, is as nought to us. How do you know what you may lose by neglecting this duty, which you think so trifling, or the blessing which its faithful performance may bring? Be sure that if you do your very best in that which is laid upon you daily, you will not be left without sufficient help when some weightier occasion arises. Give yourself to Him, fix your eye upon Him, listen to His voice, and then go on bravely and cheerfully.[1]

Ruth's Best

Ruth's story personifies this principle. Like Esther, her story is in a book of the Bible named after her. Ruth is a great example of a woman not stewing about circumstances she could not control, but instead choosing to believe, do her best, and embrace a bright future because of the faithfulness of God. Ruth was a poor young widow. She was a Moabite, a race often despised by Jews, but she did not allow her race, gender, or social status to define her. Consequently, she experienced God's favor. Psalm 84:11 says, "The Lord bestows favor and honor." It is God's prerogative to grant His favor to whomever He will.

This poor, obscure young widow, a member of a race often seen as inferior, found great favor with Jehovah God, with men, and with one special man—a wealthy one, at that. Why did God choose Ruth to go down in history as the great-grandmother of King David?

I see at least six qualities that made Ruth distinct, an attractive candidate for God's favor. The first one is faith. She was willing to step outside her comfort zone. I doubt if Ruth ever dreamed of being a widow (a young one, at that) and then moving to a foreign country, where she would be in the minority. She did not expect life after marriage to be so hard. But she had embraced the God of her husband and mother-in-law, Naomi, a God who never makes mistakes. Bound with a steadfast faith and determination, Ruth was committed to returning with Naomi to her hometown, Bethlehem, and serving her God. She had no idea what was ahead, except God. There were no guarantees. She could not undo her past, her status: single again, living on the poverty line; she couldn't change her race, but she could choose to walk by faith and follow a God who is no respecter of persons. She told Naomi, "Your people will be my people and your God my God" (Ruth 1:16).

Ruth was kind. She had a servant's heart. She demonstrated her kindness by leaving her homeland and seeing it as her responsibility to get a job to take care of not only herself but also Naomi. She was known for her kind words and deeds. In Ruth 2:2, she tells Naomi, "Let me go to the fields and pick up the leftover grain behind anyone in whose eyes I find favor." She wanted to do what she could so she took the initiative, trusting God to grant her favor with the right landowner. Israelite law demanded that any grain that was dropped was to be left for poor people to pick up. Because Ruth went looking for work, God directed her to the field of a wealthy landowner, Boaz, who was single. Ruth's kindness attracted the man. When he met Ruth, he said,

> I've been told all about what you've done for your mother-in-law since the death of your husband—how you left your father and mother and your homeland and came to live with a people you did not know before. May the Lord repay you for what you have done. May you be richly rewarded by the Lord, the God of Israel, under whose wings you have come to take refuge.
>
> Ruth 2:11–12

Ruth was not only kind but also diligent. She wasn't just a day laborer, but a hard worker. She gave it her best. In Ruth 2:7 (NLT), the foreman describes Ruth's routine to the owner, Boaz: "She asked me this morning if she could gather grain behind the harvesters. She has been hard at work ever since, except for a few minutes' rest in the shelter." The boss noticed her work ethic, and he in turn told the big boss.

What's interesting to me about Ruth is she doesn't expect God to do it all. Yes, she took a leap of faith and moved to a foreign country, but she didn't fill her days in Bethlehem with lots of pity parties or excuses, such as, "I don't know anybody," "I don't have any skills," or "I'm not from around here, so I probably won't get a job." No, she got busy doing all she could to change her situation. In Ruth 2:2, she trusted God to order her steps to the right job. She refused to dwell on things she could not change. She believed God would grant her favor with a potential boss, and He did. In Ruth 2:3, it says, "As it turned out, she was working in a field belonging to Boaz." Proverbs 20:24 says, "A person's steps are directed by the Lord."

Ruth was also humble. She had a spirit of humility, not one of pride, arrogance, or haughtiness. When wealthy Boaz took interest and gave her some preferential treatment on the job, exclusive access to his fields, Ruth 2:10 says, "At this, she bowed down with her face to the ground. She asked him, 'Why have I found such favor in your eyes that you notice me—a foreigner?'" Verse 13 continues, "'May I continue to find favor in your eyes, my lord,' she said. 'You have put me at ease by speaking kindly to your servant—though I do not have the standing of one of your servants.'"

Humility is having a proper estimation of ourselves. It's not thinking more highly of ourselves than is warranted. Ruth's attitude was not, "Boaz, I'm not surprised you noticed me. I'm a young woman. I have it going on." She saw no need to embellish her résumé. She was a secure woman because of her relationship with God. She admitted, "I do not have the standing of one of your servants." She wasn't talking about her self-worth, but her standing, her position in life. She knew the difference.

Your status or lack of it won't deprive you of God's favor.

Your status or lack of it won't deprive you of God's favor. We live in a culture that is impressed by who you are, who you know, where you live, what you do, how you look, the car you drive, and the size of your bankroll. Not God. Humility impresses Him. "Humility comes before honor" (Proverbs 18:12). Ruth expressed humility in her speech and in her tone. We can send strong and wrong messages with our harsh tone of voice. You've probably heard the statement "It's not *what* you say; it's *how* you say it." How you say it is your tone. It can either open a door or shut down the opportunity. You can sound inviting or insulting.

Ruth was not a know-it-all. She possessed a teachable spirit. She was willing to follow wise counsel. We see this quality at the end of chapter 2, when she told Naomi about her workday and her encounter with Boaz and his offer for her to glean exclusively in his field. After hearing it, Naomi told her (v. 22), "It will be good for you, my daughter, to go with the women who work for him, because in someone else's field you might be harmed." Naomi was encouraging Ruth to work only in Boaz's fields. Ruth could have responded, "I know how to take care of myself. I don't need you to tell me what to do. I get bored easily. I want to visit other fields too and see what's out there." No, it says in verse 23, "So Ruth stayed close to the women of Boaz to glean until the barley and wheat harvests were finished." Ruth did as Naomi suggested.

She also revealed a teachable attitude when Naomi coached her on how to get a man, Boaz in particular. Naomi told her about the custom in her land that would indicate to Boaz that he could be her kinsman redeemer and marry her. A kinsman redeemer was a relative who volunteered to take responsibility for the extended family.

Naomi laid out the specifics of what Ruth should do. It was practical stuff: wash up, put on perfume and her best outfit, go to his threshing floor, and uncover his feet. This action would indicate to Boaz that Ruth was available. Naomi knew that men are visual. Ruth could have recoiled and said to Naomi, "I don't need you to tell me how to get a man. I'm experienced when it comes to that. I got your son, remember? I'm grown and quite capable of getting another husband. Just watch me." Instead, Ruth told Naomi in chapter 3:5–6, "I will do whatever you say. . . . So she went down to the threshing floor and did *everything* her mother-in-law told her to do" (emphasis mine). After the mission was accomplished, Naomi told Ruth, "Wait, my daughter, until you find out what happens" (Ruth 3:18). In other words, there is no need for you to do another thing. The ball is now in Boaz's court.

In being the best she could be, Ruth was virtuous. Her godly reputation preceded her. Boaz told her, "All the people of my town know that you are a woman of noble character [or a virtuous woman]" (Ruth 3:11). Boaz was drawn to Ruth because of her character, not her clothes; her virtue, not her vices; her spirit, not her shape. When a man talks about your godly reputation, it speaks volumes. Men talk. If the word on the street is that her walk matches her talk, that's saying a lot. Boaz didn't waste any time going through the process to secure Ruth as his wife. They became ancestors of King David.

Be Authentically You

You may remember the popular television series *Mission Impossible* or the movie franchise by the same name. The program always opened with recorded instructions for the new assignment. Before the tape self-destructed, "the voice" said, "This is your assignment, if you choose to accept it."

God's assignment is a dual one (if you choose to accept it): doing your best and aspiring to be authentically you. This means accepting your uniqueness, your design. It's being true to who you are. You represent God's creativity. Think about this when you look at a variety of fruit: Bananas are yellow and lean; you have to peel them in order to eat them. A raspberry is tiny; you simply pop it into your mouth. A cherry has a pit; you have to skillfully move it to the side of your mouth or spit it out. A pear is green or yellow on the outside and shaped differently from an apple; it gets softer as it ripens. The kiwi is soft when you peel and slice it; there are tiny seeds that don't have much taste. Nothing is more succulent than tasting fruit that is fully ripe. The process getting there varies for each one.

What I find interesting is that when I eat a strawberry, I never expect it to taste like another fruit. I'm not surprised that it tastes nothing like an orange. You don't hear strawberries asking why they aren't longer and leaner like the banana or smaller like a raspberry. A watermelon doesn't go around bragging about its size. It knows being bigger doesn't make it better. The other fruits know that as well. I wouldn't touch or taste a watermelon-size blueberry. It wasn't created to be huge. No, each fruit is content to be authentically its own color, shape, size, and flavor. They don't compare, compete, or covet. They also don't expect everyone to like them. I have my favorite fruits, and there are others I never eat. I'm glad they don't take my preferences personally.

Why aren't we content to aspire to be the best-tasting fruit God made us to be? Our sphere of influence may be small yet significant. We can waste so much time comparing, competing, criticizing, complaining, and coveting. We can accomplish God's purposes in our own packaging when we make the most of what we have.

I struggled with *my* authenticity at different times in my life. I remember talking to God as a child about my height and my personality. I didn't like either. I was the tallest girl in my sixth-grade class, with only one boy taller than me. I was practically at my final height of five feet eight inches. Having six older brothers and no sisters influenced me in a unique way.

I was self-assured, with a strong personality. I wanted to be a dainty "girlie girl." I tried it for a day several times but could never pull it off. I kept asking God, *Why?* "How come I'm not like the other girls I know?" Finally one day, the Lord spoke to my heart and said, "I know what I'm doing, Cheryl. I have given you the personality you need to do what I called you to do." I was focused on the personality I wanted in hopes of being popular with the boys.

It wasn't until the Lord opened doors for a career in television, and I got the opportunity to host my own show with a roundtable of male journalists, that I realized why God wired me as He did. I felt so relaxed, right at home. It was just like I was talking to my brothers. Psalm 119:91 says, "Everything serves your plans" (NLT). I said quietly to the Lord one day, "Wow, Lord, you do know what you're doing!"

I encourage you to accept your design and embrace your God-given assignment. Be authentically you. That's when you will have your greatest success. Have you ever heard the same song sung by two different artists? The song was the same, but not the execution. Each soloist made it *his* song with a unique interpretation and voice quality. He or she "owned" it. That's what it means to be authentically you. Own your uniqueness. Celebrate it.

I encourage you to spend quality time looking inward and upward, asking God such questions as "How did you wire me?" "What's unique about me?" "What should I do to hone my gift?" "How should I use my uniqueness for your glory?" Ask friends and family members what makes you authentic. Many times, others can

Be authentically you. That's when you will have your greatest success.

see in us what we don't see in ourselves. We take it for granted.
They see it as our calling card.

You don't know your assignment? Ask God. He'll tell you.
Do your best and put your authentic imprint on it.

becoming distinctly you

1. How has God skillfully crafted you? Are you doing the best you can with your package? If not, what needs improvement?

2. Which of the three servants in the parable (Matthew 25:14–30) do you identify with and why?

3. Were you surprised that the first two servants received the same commendation for their work? What does this say about the fairness of the Master?

4. What is your takeaway from this story?

5. List the six traits of Ruth that I mentioned. Which do you admire the most? Which do you need to cultivate?

6. Why do you think God made each fruit unique?

7. How can you use your uniqueness for God's glory?

15

A Big View of God

How big is your God? What is your view of God and His power? Your opinion of God will cause Him to loom either large or small in your life. He is only as big as you see Him. Jesus could not perform many miracles in Nazareth because of unbelief. It wasn't unusual for Jesus to respond to those He healed by saying, "Your faith has made you well" (Mark 5:34; Luke 8:48 NLT). Believing faith triggered healing. To be distinct, you must believe that God is right there, committed to doing whatever it takes to fulfill His purpose for your life. This is how God describes himself in Isaiah 46:9–11:

> I am God, and there is no other; I am God, and there is none like me. I make known the end from the beginning, from ancient times, what is still to come. I say, "My purpose will stand, and I will do all that I please." . . . What I have said, that will I bring about; what I have planned, that I will do.

When Joseph's brothers were afraid that he would punish them for their malicious acts of throwing him in a pit and selling him to an Egyptian, Joseph didn't miss a beat, saying, "You intended to harm me, but God intended it for good to accomplish what is now being done, the saving of many lives" (Genesis 50:20). That is amazing. After all he had gone through (sold as a slave, wrongfully charged with rape, serving jail time), we see no record of Joseph complaining or blaming God. We don't see a trace of bitterness or resentment toward God or his brothers. Joseph did not have a small view of God. It was huge. He firmly believed in his God-given dream, that his father and brothers would one day serve him. At His appointed time, God showed up in a big way, doing something He had never done before. Joseph went from being a prisoner to a prime minister (with no steps in between). Only a sovereign God could orchestrate that. On cue, He rescued Joseph from his horrible, unfair ordeal.

Have you studied what God has said? That's what He will do. If we make it a priority to study God's Word intently, it will solve many of our problems. We would know God's will because He has already decreed that everything He said is what He is going to do. There are more than seven thousand promises in the Bible. How many do you know and believe? It is impossible for God to lie. Unfortunately, we are quick to take people at their word and totally discount what God says. We are shocked when they disappoint us, yet God says, "Those who hope in me will not be disappointed" (Isaiah 49:23). Faith is taking God at His word and standing on it, no matter what.

How do you develop your faith muscle and a big view of God? "Faith comes from hearing, that is, hearing the Good News about Christ" (Romans 10:17 NLT). The more we saturate ourselves in the Word of God and allow it to penetrate our minds and our hearts, the more our faith in God will rise. Notice I said faith in *God*. We live in a culture that encourages us to look inward to build up our self-confidence. That's not how it works in God's kingdom. He says, "Believe in me. Have faith in me. Never doubt me. I am able to do exceeding abundantly above all you could ever ask or think, but it's according to the power that works in you" (see Ephesians 3:20). That power is an unmovable faith in God. It is available to every person who believes. One thing moves God, and it is faith. That is, trusting Him, despite the odds. God is big enough to move any obstacle. Do you believe that? In order to be distinct, you must believe that nothing and no one can thwart the will of God.

All of the amazing things that have happened in my life are because I had a big view of God. Not a big view of myself, but God. There is absolutely nothing that God cannot do. One day the Lord spoke to me and said, "Cheryl, I want to prove myself mighty to this generation of Christians, but my hands are tied because of their unbelief. They don't think I can do it. They don't bother to ask. I can only be as big as they see me. I am still the same, the God of Isaac, Jacob, Joseph, Elijah, and Elisha. I have not changed. I'm waiting for someone to believe me."

Having a big view of God causes us to rest, not rant, when life doesn't go our way.

I am determined to be that person. Almost on a daily basis I recite this truth: "The God of Abraham, Isaac, Jacob, Joseph, Daniel, Esther, Ruth, Peter, and Paul is my God. He is orchestrating my life. He is my source, my peace, my wisdom, my provider, my shepherd. And He has already given me everything I need for life and godliness" (see 2 Peter 1:3 KJV). I say it until it becomes a part of my inner being. I say it before I'm in trouble. I get a head start on doubt and fear.

When I think of someone having a big view of God, Mary is at the top of the list. Here she was a poor teenager, making plans to marry Joseph. Nothing appeared to be special about her, but God saw differently. He had a distinct plan for her life. What was about to happen to her had never happened before to anyone. It would go down in the history books. Mary didn't have a clue, but on the appointed day, God sent the angel Gabriel to Nazareth with a special message for her. Please remember that Gabriel didn't miss his exit and end up at the wrong place. This assignment was tailor-made for one woman. I bring this up because so many times we can want something or someone so badly, and it looks like it's ours or he's our mate, and then something happens and we don't get the opportunity or the man. Someone else does, and we are mad at God and the world. What happened? Were they smarter, was she prettier or younger? Having a big view of God causes us to rest, not rant, when life doesn't go our way. He is in charge of the opened doors as well as closed doors. He doesn't make a mistake either way. Our Father knows best. He will not give your blessing to someone else. He knows where you live. Gabriel went to the right house, and he didn't need a video or a photo of Mary to find her.

Gabriel said to Mary, "Greetings, you who are highly favored! The Lord is with you. . . . Do not be afraid, Mary; you have found favor with God. You will conceive and give birth to a son, and you are to call him Jesus. He will be great and will be called the Son of the Most High" (Luke 1:28–32). What does this declaration tell me about Mary? She knew God and God knew her. In her song called the *Magnificat* (Luke 1:46–55), Mary spoke of God's mercy, mighty deeds, and help to Abraham and his descendants. Mary had gained God's favor. What's more important to you? God's favor, or your friends' favor?

Mary asked one question: "How will this be, since I'm a virgin?" It wasn't a question of doubt but of process. The angel answered, "The Holy Spirit will come on you, and the power of the Most High will overshadow you. . . . For no word from God will ever fail" (Luke 1:34–37). What was Mary's response? One of submission to God's distinct plan for her. She said, "I am the Lord's servant . . . may your word to me be fulfilled" (v. 38). God had spoken and that settled it.

I'm certain Mary had some plans of her own, but after she heard from the angel what God's plan was for her, she acquiesced. God's ways are not our ways; neither are His thoughts our thoughts (Isaiah 55:8). This is why I am not a huge proponent of spending huge chunks of time plotting our lives and then praying for God to work things out the way we envision. I don't find this approach in Scripture. I find that God shows up on an ordinary day when you're doing your ordinary tasks, and He pronounces what His will is through ordinary circumstances. Your path crosses with someone at the airport or at the store. It is a divine connection. One thing leads to another. When you are consumed with *your* goals, *your* plans, and *your* dreams it can be difficult to release them when God shows up with another agenda. He is always full of surprises and never works the way we dream. Release wasn't difficult for Mary because she identified herself as the "Lord's servant." A servant doesn't call the shots; the Master does. A servant has one agenda: doing the Master's assignments. Mary's life was not her own. She understood the meaning of servanthood.

Mary also had a big view of God because she trusted emphatically what the angel said. She knew that when God decrees something, He covers all the bases. We don't see her asking the angel, "What should I tell Joseph? What if he doesn't believe me? What are people going to say? People are going to think Joseph and I fooled around. I can't face my parents. I will be stoned." If she had played the "what if" game, she would have been depressed and traumatized thinking about all the possible scenarios. She left all the details, including her reputation, in God's hands. After all, this was *His* plan. She rested in His sovereignty. When Mary ran to the town where her cousin Elizabeth (who was pregnant with John the Baptist) lived to spend time with her, Elizabeth exclaimed, "God has blessed you above all women, and your child is blessed. . . . You are blessed because you *believed* that the Lord would do what he said" (Luke 1:42, 45 NLT, emphasis mine).

When you are consumed with your goals, your plans, and your dreams it can be difficult to release them when God shows up with another agenda.

Mary had a *big* view of God. Her belief in God fueled her blessing. According to Elizabeth, she was blessed because she believed—not because she was the most beautiful or the brightest, but because she took God at His Word.

I will never forget God looming large in my life while I was in graduate school. It was a requirement for the broadcast students to spend a quarter in Washington, DC, serving as a correspondent for a local television station in a small market. I was assigned to be the Washington reporter for the NBC affiliate station in Peoria, Illinois. One day I noticed that a few of my peers were whispering and working on their résumés. I thought, *This is strange. We just got to DC, and we still have another quarter to go after this one. It's too early to be job hunting. Something is up.* I didn't know what it was, so I prayed. I distinctly remember praying silently at my desk, saying, "Lord, something is going on here, and I don't know what it is, but I'm confident that if it's something I'm supposed to be a part of, you will make sure that happens." I never prayed about it again.

A couple of weeks later, I missed an important story deadline for my station. I was devastated. When I returned to our news bureau, I went in to talk with my instructor about it. I was in tears. We chatted for a while, but it was getting late so she suggested we continue to talk while we took the subway. We got on the subway, and it broke down (that had never happened to me before), so we continued to talk. These were the longest conversations we'd ever had. I didn't realize it then, but our talk became a turning point in how my instructor viewed me. I was quiet in class. I just did my work. She didn't really know me personally until that day.

Several weeks later, my instructor called me into her office and asked me to close the door. She said, "Cheryl, I have something to tell you. You have really blossomed in these last few weeks, demonstrating true growth. I now see you in a different light. At the beginning of the quarter, NBC News contacted the journalism school and asked us to recommend our top students to interview for the NBC Associates program. Your professors back in Evanston had selected you, but I told them that I didn't see in you what they did, so I did not recommend you. I have felt so bad about this the last few weeks, so this is what I did. I contacted NBC and asked if they could interview one more student. Here's the phone number. You need to call immediately to get a slot, because the first interviews will take place here in DC in the next week or so."

As she was telling me this, I was thinking, *God, you have answered my prayer. God, you have answered my prayer. You did this!* I'm so glad He did it this way. I couldn't take the credit. If my instructor had selected me in the beginning, chances are a twinge of pride would have shown up along with an attitude of entitlement. This way, only God could get the credit.

My mother and I prayed fervently, dependent on God's favor as I went through each round of interviews. The program consisted of two reporter trainee positions at the local NBC affiliate television stations in Milwaukee and Nashville. The network would pay the salary for a year.

I made the cut of the first interviews. The next step was to interview with four news vice-presidents at the NBC headquarters in New York City. I enjoyed talking to each of them. It was hard to believe I was at NBC News. This exceeded my wildest dreams. My mother and I kept praying because we believed that God had orchestrated this. So we were stunned when I found out I didn't get either of the positions. One went to a peer, and the other went to a guy who already worked for the network in an entry-level position. My mother and I discussed this, and we refused to believe it was over. *Why would God bring me this far and then not give me the job?* It didn't make sense. We kept praying.

A couple of weeks later I got a call from the network. The person on the other end said, "We have just created a third position at our local station in Washington. It's a fifteen-month assignment. It won't be reporting, but rather working with the station's political correspondent. Are you interested in interviewing for this job?" I said, "Sure." I made the first cut of interviews with the news managers. It was down to two candidates. The correspondent, Susan, would make the final decision after interviewing both of us. By this time I was back on the Evanston campus, so I had to fly to Washington for the interview. I remember praying all along the way that God would grant me favor if this was His will.

I thought the interview with Susan went well. It was natural, effortless. I prayed on the plane heading back home, acknowledging my dependence on God. Several days later I got the job offer. My big God had come through for me. This job brought me to Washington, and all of my subsequent broadcasting jobs have been here. This is unusual; most journalists typically work in several smaller markets before obtaining a position in a large metropolitan area.

When I arrived at the station, the news director said to me, "I know you have an interest in being a reporter, but don't even think about it happening here." I took his words to heart. I knew my assignment. It was to assist Susan. That's what I concentrated on, giving it my best. We had a great working relationship. I learned so much from her. I enjoyed traveling with her on the presidential campaign trail. While we were covering the Pennsylvania primary, Susan said to me, "Why don't you write a couple of stories as if you were the reporter. You can use my video, and my camera operator can shoot your on-camera stand-ups." I said, "Okay." When she saw the finished product, she said, "I think you should send these to the executives in New York." I did. After their review, they called the news director (yes, the same news director who told me not to think about becoming a reporter there) and told him to put me on the air, and the network would extend my assignment and pay my salary for another year. Who could orchestrate this but God? I was going on-air as a reporter in one of the top-ten television markets. Most reporters have to work years in the business before getting there. God had other plans.

becoming distinctly
you

1. Which is more important to you, God's favor or your friends' favor? How is this evident in your choices?

2. How can reading God's Word elevate your view of God?

3. Read Luke 1:26–38. What impresses you the most about Mary's response to this incredible news?

4. Read Luke 1:42, 45. What role does believing play in God looming large in our lives?

5. "You can have as much of God as you want." Do you believe that? If so, how much do you want?

—— *Nugget* ——

Develop the habit of declaring this truth: "The God of Abraham, Isaac, Jacob, Ruth, Mary, and Elizabeth is my God. He has not changed. He is still all-powerful. He is just as committed to proving himself mighty in my life as He was for them. My job is to believe. Lord, I believe."

16

Focus

When you are determined to be distinct, you will focus on God's leading. We live in a culture that specializes in attempts to drown out God's voice. We face distractions from the moment we wake up. Our cell phones are ringing, we need to check emails, surf the Internet, text, review our Facebook and Twitter pages, download photos, post on Instagram and Pinterest, not to mention work a full-time job, be an engaging wife and mother, prepare meals on the run, and keep the house clean.

Many voices are vying for our attention, but which is most important? It is tuning our ears to the heavenly frequency WGOD. It is critical to cultivate the art of listening to God's voice, recognizing when He speaks. Do we answer His calls, respond to His text messages? He wants us to be *His* fan. The key to our impact, to our success, to all of our needs being met, and to making the most of each season of our lives, is knowing His voice and responding. Jesus said in John 10:27, "My sheep listen to my voice; I know them, and they follow me."

Sharpening this skill is at the top of my to-do list. I need more aptitude in this area, because when I look at any of the poor, bad, or dumb decisions I have made, I can trace them back to one of three things: either I did not take the time to consult God, I was confused and thought God told me to do something and realized later He didn't, or I knew God's voice but elected to do what I wanted to do instead. I confess I am and will always be a sheep in desperate need of a shepherd. It has nothing to do with age. David made the same declaration in Psalm 23: "The Lord is my shepherd. . . . He guides me along the right paths" (vv. 1, 3). In Psalm 5:8 (NLT), David prays, "Lead me in the right path, O Lord." In Psalm 25:4, he says, "Show me your ways, Lord, teach me your paths."

As one minister told me, "Everything you need in life to accomplish God's purposes for you is on your path—everything!" That includes joy, wisdom, career connections, fulfillment, provisions, and your ideal mate if marriage is God's will for you. It's like following the yellow-brick road. If you stay on it, it will lead you to your God-given destiny. That's why we need to focus. Unwavering trust in God and not in ourselves gives us focus. "Trust in the Lord with all your heart and lean not on your own understanding; in all your ways acknowledge him, and he will make your paths straight. Do not be wise in your own eyes; fear the Lord and shun evil" (Proverbs 3:5–7). We can only trust God wholeheartedly when we empty ourselves of our knowledge, our intellect. I remind myself constantly, "Cheryl, do not be wise in your own eyes. Don't lean on your own understanding. You will get in trouble if you have a high opinion of your knowledge."

Jesus is our perfect example of undeterred focus. He was obsessed with one goal: to do His Father's will. He never did something just because He could. He had the power to heal every person in town, but He didn't. He could have started His earthly ministry earlier, but He didn't. It helps our focus to regularly review *His* focus:

> My nourishment comes from doing the will of God, who sent me, and from finishing his work.
>
> John 4:34 NLT

> I can do nothing on my own. I judge as God tells me.
>
> John 5:30 NLT

> For I have come down from heaven to do the will of God who sent me, not to do my own will.
>
> John 6:38 NLT

> I live because of the living Father who sent me.
>
> John 6:57 NLT

> My message is not my own; it comes from God who sent me.
>
> John 7:16 NLT

> For I say only what I have heard from the one who sent me, and he is completely truthful.
>
> John 8:26 NLT

> I do nothing on my own but say only what the Father taught me. . . . For I always do what pleases him.
>
> John 8:28–29 NLT

Can you imagine the impact if every card-carrying Christ follower had one agenda every day: to only say and do what pleased the Father? That's being distinct.

This kind of focus requires daily fighting the flesh. The flesh wants to kick back and take the easy route, the one without a struggle. This road will not lead to distinctiveness. The apostle Paul said in 1 Corinthians 9:27, "I strike a blow to my body and make it my slave so that after I have preached to others, I myself will not be disqualified for the prize." This verse comes to my mind almost every morning before I get out of bed. It reminds me of my responsibility to make my mind, and my body, conform to all the Word I know. That's a full-time job, because I know a lot of the Word. The devil is the dean of distractions. Paul cautioned believers,

Jesus is our perfect example of undeterred focus.

> Be strong in the Lord and in his mighty power. Put on all of God's armor so that you will be able to stand firm against all strategies of the devil. For we are not fighting against flesh-and-blood enemies, but against evil rulers and authorities of the unseen world, against mighty powers of this dark world, and against evil spirits in the heavenly places.
>
> Ephesians 6:10–12 NLT

My Old Testament model for focus and diligence is Nehemiah. He distinguished himself by fulfilling a God-given dream in a record amount of time: fifty-two days. Nehemiah was a government worker in a foreign country, Persia. He had a prestigious position with direct access to the king as his trusted cupbearer. His job was to ensure that everything the king ate and drank was safe and of top quality. If it wasn't, it would mean curtains for Nehemiah. He was well respected and flourished on his job. But Nehemiah had a dream: to be a problem solver and return to his homeland, Jerusalem, to lead an effort to rebuild the city's walls. They had been in shambles for seventy years. He got reports that the walls were broken down and the gates burned. This was a disgrace back then because walls around cities were essential. They represented protection and prestige. Nehemiah was filled with compassion, but before he could take action, he focused on praying. He decided not to do anything without looking inward and getting his life right with God first. You probably won't find this action step in any of the *New York Times* bestselling business books, but it's in God's Book. Nehemiah wept, fasted, prayed, and poured his heart out to God about his deficiencies before he got to his desire and dream. Nehemiah 1:4–7 says,

> For some days I mourned and fasted and prayed before the God of heaven. Then I said: "Lord, the God of heaven, the great and awesome God, who keeps his covenant of love with those who love him and keep his commandments, let your ear be attentive and your eyes open to hear the prayer your servant is praying before you day and night for your servants, the people of Israel. I confess the sins we Israelites, including myself and my father's family, have committed against you. We have acted very wickedly toward you. We have not obeyed the commands, decrees and laws you gave your servant Moses."

Did you notice that the first thing out of Nehemiah's mouth was not a prayer for God to bless his plans or his dream? No, he approached God with reverential awe and fear. He displayed humility and brokenness. He spent time fasting and soul searching. He confessed his sins, acknowledging that he had disobeyed God's laws. He recognized that before he could ask God to bless his dream, he had to come clean. We can't expect God to sanction and bless our goals and desires when we are walking in disobedience to His will. We can't skip over that. God doesn't.

After Nehemiah confessed his sins and repented, he asked the Lord to hear his prayer for success with the project. He said, "O Lord . . . please grant me success today by making the king favorable to me. Put it into his heart to be kind to me" (Nehemiah 1:11 NLT).

After praying, Nehemiah turned his focus to preparing and planning. Some time after his initial prayers regarding his passion, Nehemiah had the opportunity to ask his boss, the king, for his help. God set it up that way. One day the king noticed that Nehemiah had a sad countenance. That was a no-no in the king's presence. He asked Nehemiah what the problem was and what he wanted. Before Nehemiah answered, he said a quick prayer in his mind, and then shared his plan. Prayer was always his first reflex. I believe he had thought it through before the king asked him what was bothering him.

God prompted the king to ask Nehemiah a question, and he was ready to make wise use of this once-in-a-lifetime opportunity. Nehemiah shared his plan with the king. He spoke respectfully to his boss and asked him to allow him to return to Jerusalem so he could rebuild the walls. The king asked him how long it would take and when he would return. Nehemiah didn't say, "Um, I don't know. I hadn't thought it through. You caught me off guard. I'll get back to you on that." Nehemiah gave the king a set time. He also asked for letters of recommendation. He knew exactly what he needed and was ready for the task. He was prepared. Nehemiah 2:8 says, "And because the gracious hand of my God was upon me, the king granted my requests." Nehemiah had God's favor, and God touched the king's heart. The king gave Nehemiah more than he asked for: the letters of recommendation, plus army officers and a cavalry to accompany him.

Nehemiah had prayed, planned, and prepared, so he expected and waited for God's provision through providential circumstances. When a dream or vision is of God, you can always count on the providential circumstances lining up. Nehemiah's boss was a blessing, not an impediment. If the king had said, "No, I can't give you a leave of absence or any assistance," then it would be clear to Nehemiah that this was either not God's timing or not God's project for him to oversee. We should not overlook this key principle. God works through our circumstances. You may believe that God told you that a certain man is to be your husband. The only problem is, he doesn't like you, is not attracted to you, and avoids you. You never have to force a door open when God is at work. He is in the details. See Him in closed doors as well as open doors. We are so quick to acknowledge God's hand when our idea is supported or our dream realized, but we can be prone to disappointment when there is no movement in our direction. The sovereign God is still at work, shielding us from what is *not* His will.

Isn't it great to have the forces of heaven involved in the details of our lives? God doesn't want us to make a mistake any more than we do. We would be wise to acknowledge and accept all closed doors. I came to this conclusion after not getting a job with *60 Minutes*. I was told about an opening as an associate producer on the venerable news magazine show. I immediately thought, *This must be God. It would be so prestigious to work for* 60 Minutes. I applied and had an interview, which I thought went well. In the interim, I was praying feverishly for God's favor with the decision makers and trusting that I would be selected. I had done all I could do. I even bargained with God, telling Him I would give Him all the glory and honor if I got this job. I would have no room for pride.

Days later I got a call from the woman who interviewed me. She said, "You were a strong candidate and came very close to being selected, but we chose someone else." I hung up the phone, got in the middle of my bed, and just cried, and cried, and cried. I really wanted that job. I did the mental check off: I prayed, sought God, asked for His favor, had a great interview, and didn't get it. Finally, after I was done crying and God could get through to me, He said softly, "Cheryl, in the process, you never *asked* me if this job was my will for you. You just *assumed* it was because it was a great opportunity and you wanted it."

What could I say? God was right. I had been focused on achieving my will, and thinking my will had to be His will. *Wrong.* Not everything that looks good or ideal is necessarily God's will. Conversely, something that looks difficult or undesirable could be His will. Seeking His direction on the front end—without having our own agenda—helps to clarify God's purpose for us. God knows that one decision we make can totally change the course of our lives. That position would have put me exclusively on the producer track. God still wanted me on the on-air anchor/host track. Over time, I was glad that God said a firm no to my desires.

Not everything that looks good or ideal is necessarily God's will.

152

If you experience providential circumstances as a confirmation, then proceed. Walk through every open door with God-confidence. I made the mistake of not doing so when I got that unexpected promotion to be an on-air reporter. I knew that God had provided this wonderful opportunity, one I had never imagined. I started reporting, eventually doing stories for the coveted 11 p.m. newscast. But then two things happened: We got a new news director who didn't particularly care for me, and several of my colleagues resented the fact that I was now on-air. They had paid their dues; I had not. Rather than focusing on God and His provision, I began to listen to the naysayers and internalize their negative attitudes. I lost confidence in myself and my ability. My self-talk turned to "I don't deserve this. I am not qualified." I was ripe for failure. Just like Peter. He walked on water as long as he kept his eyes on his Savior. As soon as he focused inwardly and on the impossibility of what he was doing, he failed. My inner insecurity soon impacted my outward demeanor. People can tell when you are not confident. You are vulnerable. I was still doing the work, but it wasn't long before I was called into the general manager's office for the separation agreement. I will never forget one thing he said to me: "Would you really want to stay and work in an environment where your work is never viewed as good enough to lead the newscast?" A perception had set in. It was time to move on.

Years later, the Lord rewound the videotape of that job. He said, "You had *me* on your side, but you started doubting that you could do the assignment that I had given you and that you had been doing for over a year." I have never forgotten that lesson. I should have worked harder and remained extremely confident, not because I was the best, but because it was God who had provided the opportunity, and He always gives us what we need when we trust Him and keep our eyes focused on Him.

Nehemiah moved forward and arrived in Jerusalem. He proceeded with caution. He kept his ideas for rebuilding to himself until the appropriate time. There is a time to speak and a time to keep silent. You can't tell your vision to everyone. That person may block your dreams or beat you to them. Nehemiah 2:12 says, "I had not told anyone what my God had put in my heart to do for Jerusalem." Then verse 16 says, "The officials did not know where I had gone or what I was doing, because as yet I had said nothing to the Jews or the priests or nobles or officials or any others who would be doing the work."

Once he started the rebuilding project with a team, Nehemiah met opposition with two ringleaders: Sanballat and Tobiah. "When Sanballat heard that we were rebuilding the wall, he became angry and was greatly incensed. He ridiculed the Jews" (Nehemiah 4:1). He and his friends plotted to fight against them. Nehemiah and his team's response? They remained focused, persevered, and prayed. They prayed and they worked with all their hearts. Nehemiah told his team, "Don't be afraid of them. Remember the Lord, who is great and awesome" (v. 14). "Our God will fight for us" (v. 20).

To be distinct, we must persevere. Just because God is in it doesn't mean it will be easy. I have a plaque that reads, "Faith makes things possible, not easy." That was Nehemiah's testimony.

Opposition can come from within or without. You might be afraid because you know you're in over your head, the economy is tight, and you have enemies. That's the time to rehearse over and over, with assurance, that you are doing what God told you to do. You got confirmation from God first before you got started, and this was His idea. Then you can say confidently, like Nehemiah, "God *will* give me success."

When Nehemiah's enemies saw the progress in rebuilding the wall, they tried a new tactic. They sent a message to Nehemiah saying, "Come, let us meet together in one of the villages on the plain of Ono" (Nehemiah 6:2). But Nehemiah was determined to stay focused on the task at hand. The wall was near completion. "But they were scheming to harm me; so I sent messengers to them with this reply: 'I am carrying on a great project and cannot go down. Why should the work stop while I leave it and go down to you?'" (vv. 2–3). They attempted to interrupt his concentration five times with various schemes. None of them worked because Nehemiah kept the main thing the main thing. He and his team kept praying and working in the strength of the Lord. They completed the wall in a record fifty-two days! The naysayers said it couldn't be done, but God said otherwise. I love what Nehemiah says in verse 16: "When all our enemies heard about this, all the surrounding nations were afraid and lost their self-confidence, because they realized that this work had been done with the help of our God."

Do you see the significance of that statement? That same God wants to work in our lives today in such a way that when we succeed, when we are distinct, it is not about us, not about our bragging rights, but it's an opportunity to put Him on display *big time*. He wants the entire world to see that our distinctive work is because He is on our side. Are you ready to focus?

becoming distinctly
you

1. What is your game plan for resisting distractions?

2. Where should you concentrate your focus?

3. Review Jesus' focus. How does this guide you in setting priorities?

4. What difference would it make in your life if your daily to-do list always pleased God?

5. Read 1 Corinthians 9:27. How does it apply to your life?

6. Read Ephesians 6:10–18. Name the pieces of armor to be worn daily.

7. In Nehemiah's prayer, he acknowledged his shortcomings first before asking God to honor his desires and grant him success with the king. Why was this essential?

17

Limit Limitations

You are experiencing at least one obstacle or limitation on the road to distinctive because no person or circumstance is perfect. What's yours? Is it your age, color, gender, health, looks, disability, abuse, IQ, enemies, lack of education or money? God has decreed a specific path for you to follow in order to accomplish your destiny. What is there to fear? God will always prevail. He was well aware of your obstacles before He chose you for the assignment. Your limitation does not limit God. What's the best way to deal with it? Acknowledge it, but don't let it define you. "Limit" your limitation.

It is natural to focus on what we are not, what we don't have, what someone did to us, or what we don't know. The reasons can stack up for why we are not thriving physically, spiritually, professionally, or economically. Drop them. Why? If the limitation or obstacle is something you cannot control or change, it will not hinder you from being all God wants you to be and to do. He always makes a way. The apostle Paul said, "I can do *everything* through Christ, who gives me strength" (Philippians 4:13 NLT, emphasis mine). This means everything God wants us to do, He is committed to equipping and enabling us to do despite the odds. *Everything.* Titus 2:14 says, "He [Jesus] gave his life to free us from every kind of sin, to cleanse us, and to make us his very own people, totally committed to doing good deeds" (NLT).

I needed braces on my teeth. Four top front teeth were crooked and I had an under-bite. I didn't think much about it, since most of the kids in my neighborhood had crooked teeth. I was in the majority. My perspective changed my freshman year in college. I became close friends with Betty, who lived in the dorm room next to mine. She was cute and petite with a perfect set of teeth. She had a thing about teeth. Whenever she saw someone with a beautiful set, she raved about them. Because I hung out with Betty, I soon started noticing teeth, including mine. I influenced her to accept Christ, and she influenced me to seek orthodontic work. I'd never considered it before, but I thought, *I do plan to have a career in broadcasting, so I need to get my teeth ready for TV. I can't go on television with crooked teeth.* I became self-conscious about my teeth and smile.

Soon I shared this need with my mother. By this time she had closed the beauty shop in the back of the house and was doing "sitting" work in the homes of elderly patients. My mother saw my need and used her paycheck to finance my braces. I found an orthodontist in my college town, and in my sophomore year I was fitted for braces. He told me that if I followed his instructions perfectly, the braces should be off in time for graduation. I did everything he told me to do. I was not self-conscious at all about wearing braces in college. The timing was perfect for me. Most kids get them in elementary school or junior high. We didn't have the money then, and I didn't see the need then. I did now, and my mother was in a position to afford them. A few days before graduation, the braces came off and my teeth looked perfect. I often get compliments on my teeth and my smile. I'm not sure I would have gotten hired as a news anchor with my crooked teeth. God knew what I needed and when.

I've noticed that many times in the Bible when a person came to God complaining about a limitation or obstacle, God turned the focus to His might and power, what He could do, not the impediment. In John, chapter 5, Jesus encountered a man who had been lame for thirty-eight years. Jesus asked him one question: "Do you want to get well?" (v. 6). The man was so focused on his longtime limitation that he didn't answer the question, but defined himself by his *Your limitation does not limit God.* obstacles. "I have no one to help me into the pool when the water is stirred. While I am trying to get in, someone else goes down ahead of me" (v. 7). He saw only one way to be healed, but he was blocked every time. He viewed his situation as hopeless. Jesus didn't waste His words discussing the obstacles. He commanded the man to pick up his mat and walk. "At once the man was cured; he picked up his mat and walked" (v. 9). That's the kind of power that indwells our Lord. It doesn't matter what we're fighting internally or externally. With one word He can change our outlook or situation or provide the grace to sustain it.

We have so many wonderful examples of Christians who have served God with what easily could be called limitations or obstacles. The great hymn writer Fanny Crosby was not born blind. It happened as a result of a mistake at the hands of her physician. She served God joyfully and wrote more than eight thousand hymns. This was her perspective at age eight, captured in her first poem:

> Oh, what a happy soul I am,
> Although I cannot see,
> I am resolved that in this world
> Contented I will be.
>
> How many blessings I enjoy
> That other people don't!
> To weep and sigh because I'm blind
> I cannot and I won't.[1]

Joni Eareckson Tada was injured in a diving accident in 1967. It left her a quadriplegic, yet she paints, writes books, records albums, and heads up one of the leading ministries for the disabled. Australian Nick Vujicic was born with no arms or legs. He's a bestselling author and one of the top inspirational speakers in the country, telling thousands about the love of Christ, to dream big, and to never lose hope. His dream to be a husband and father came true.

David Ring was born with cerebral palsy. Orphaned at age fourteen, he faced one obstacle after another. Today he calls himself a victor, not a victim. He's in full-time ministry, sharing his story of God's redemption and hope with more than a hundred thousand people a year. He is a husband, father, and grandfather. David loves to ask people this question: "I have cerebral palsy. What's your problem?" Bible teacher Joyce Meyer has candidly shared her nightmare of being sexually molested by her biological father until she left home. God gave her the grace to provide for her aging parents and to forgive her dad. He gave his life to Christ. Joyce had the privilege of baptizing him. She admits that she probably would not have the ministry she has today if she had not gone through that horrific experience of abuse.[2]

Don't run away from your limitations. Instead, embrace them, because it could be that God wants to show up and show you a more creative way of accomplishing His purposes. Limitations never stop God from being God. They amplify His distinctiveness.

becoming distinctly
you

1. What obstacles or limitations are you facing on the road to distinction? Are they defining you? If so, how?

2. How can you learn to embrace your obstacles?

3. Are you more focused on the limitations or how God can transform them into opportunities for His glory?

4. Search the Scriptures for examples of those who faced huge obstacles while being in the will of God. Write down how God came through in spite of the roadblocks.

5. Memorize Philippians 4:13. Develop the habit of saying regularly, "Despite _____, with the power and strength of Christ, I can forge ahead, and I will."

18

Adjust Your Attitude

Whenlife doesn't go as planned, it's time for a serious attitude tune-up, an adjustment. Poet and author Maya Angelou said, "If you don't like something, change it. If you can't change it, change your attitude." It's easy to waste time wallowing in mistakes or setbacks. It's okay to assess what went wrong and why and determine to learn from the experience, but then quickly make the necessary adjustments and move forward.

Relinquish the Script

I've gotten in trouble because I'm a planner and I love to fantasize about various options. I must constantly remind myself to let the script go. It's important to have total confidence that God is going to work on our behalf, but *not* write the script of *how* He's going to do it. Moses thought he was being a deliverer when he killed an Egyptian. He was acting out of his flesh and not out of God's leading. God had a bigger idea.

You don't have to relinquish your expectations if you expect from God, not people. Psalm 62:5–6 says, "My soul, wait thou only upon God; for my expectation is from him. He only is my rock and my salvation: he is my defense; I shall not be moved" (KJV). God will work in His own time and in His own way.

I experienced this firsthand the summer after my junior year of college. I was interested in religious broadcasting and asked one of my professors if he knew of any programs or internships. He told me about a summer program at the Catholic Radio & TV Centre in Middlesex, England. I had never been abroad, so I was excited about this opportunity. I also heard about a paid internship in advertising for the summer. I was torn. What should I do? Only God knew. I began to pray, and I weighed my options. When I told one well-meaning Christian about my dilemma, he quickly said, "One, you will make money, and the other you will lose money, and you don't know which one to take?" Fortunately, I had learned by experience to bathe my decisions in prayer. The logical answer is not always God's answer. After much praying, I sensed that it was God's will for me to enroll in the program in England. I knew how much money I needed. I wasn't sure where I was going to get it, but I believed I had heard from God.

A week before the trip I still didn't have the money. That Friday night I stretched out on the floor, crying out to God, telling Him (as if He didn't know) that I didn't have the money. What was I going to do? "I thought this was your will," I said. He reminded me I did not need the money that day. I got up and went on my way. A week later, when I needed the money, I had the *exact* amount I believed I needed for the trip. Why did

I ever doubt? God has an impeccable sense of timing. What I remember about that experience is from the time I boarded the plane until I returned home I had an incredible sense of God's presence. No one was traveling with me, but I knew God was with me every step of the way.

When I arrived at the London airport, I needed to take a train to my destination. I had two huge suitcases (back then I didn't know how to pack for foreign travel). Along the way, an older gentleman offered to help me with my luggage at the train station. I was so grateful for his assistance. That following Sunday, I attended a small church in the area recommended by my pastor, who did a lot of traveling for his missions work. When I walked into the church, the man who assisted me with my luggage was there. All I could do was praise God for being mindful of me by sending a wonderful Christian man to help His struggling daughter.

Be Flexible

When life doesn't go as planned, it helps to adjust your attitude and put it on *F* for flexibility. This can take a lot of practice if you are accustomed to everything going your way or you fight to be in the driver's seat. When you are flexible, you are pliable, easy to bend without breaking, willing or disposed to yielding. This is an attractive trait because it means you are open to another point of view, a different option. There is usually a stalemate when both parties are intractable, refusing to compromise. Having a dose of humility helps with flexibility, because you are not thinking of yourself or your position higher than is warranted. You go into the meeting open to other ideas. You don't assume that you have all the answers.

Adjusting your attitude does not call for being flexible on the absolutes of Scripture, but on the gray areas, where it's left to personal preference. Ask yourself, "Is this a battle worth fighting?" "What can I change in this proposal and still remain true to the concept?" "Will it really make that much of a difference if we leave at 7:30 instead of 7:00?"

Can you accept that God has chosen someone else to do what you have always dreamed of doing? You sized her up, and from your perspective, you were more gifted and talented, more diligent, more deserving and passionate, and yet she got the opportunity. Were you secretly mad or glad? The road to distinction requires an attitude adjustment, because no matter how hard you prayed or desired it, you understand and trust God's plan and acknowledge that He's not obligated to share with you all the reasons you didn't get it. You must trust His apportionment.

That's what Elizabeth did. She had a deep longing in her heart for a child, but now she was very old. Both she and her husband were from a godly lineage and pleased God with their lives. "[Zechariah and Elizabeth] were righteous in the sight of God, observing all of the Lord's commands and decrees blamelessly" (Luke 1:6). She could have wondered over the years, "Lord, why haven't you blessed me with the one thing I desire, a child? My husband and I have always put you first and served you with our whole hearts. Why are you denying us this one thing?" But we don't see this attitude in Elizabeth.

On an unexpected day when Zechariah was performing his assigned duties in the temple, the angel Gabriel appeared. He said,

> God has heard your prayer. Your wife, Elizabeth, will give you
> a son, and you are to name him John. You will have great joy
> and gladness, and many will rejoice at his birth, for he will be

great in the eyes of the Lord. . . . He will be filled with the Holy Spirit, even before his birth.

Luke 1:13–15 NLT

God was true to His word:

Soon afterward his wife, Elizabeth, became pregnant and went into seclusion for five months. "How kind the Lord is!" she exclaimed. "He has taken away my disgrace of having no children!"

Luke 1:24–25 NLT

Elizabeth and her husband had continued to pray while she was infertile. We don't see them blaming God, but blessing Him and remaining true to their calling even though year after year their heartfelt prayers went unanswered. They had no idea that the answer to their prayer was tied to the timing of the birth of the Messiah. Elizabeth couldn't give birth to the forerunner to the Messiah in her teens or twenties, before the mother of the Messiah was born! We just don't have all the details while we are waiting for God to work. His distinct plan is explicit and His timing is impeccable. Elizabeth maintained an excellent attitude, being faithful to the Lord in what she was called to do.

We just don't have all the details while we are waiting for God to work.

Her positive attitude did not change once she found out that her much younger relative, Mary, was also pregnant with a child and was carrying the Son of God. She was overjoyed at the news. After Gabriel had visited Mary with the news of her miraculous pregnancy, she hurried to Elizabeth's hometown to spend quality time with her. Elizabeth exhibited no envy. She didn't say to God, "Now, don't get me wrong. I am happy to be pregnant at this age. People are shocked that I'm this old and pregnant. So am I. But I have been serving you so much longer than Mary, and she's not married. You can attest that my husband and I have been walking upright before you our entire marriage. I was excited when you told me my son would be the forerunner of the Messiah, but that was before I found out Mary was chosen to be the Messiah's mother. She's just a teenager. Um, God, I was just wondering why you didn't pick me for this coveted position of being the mother of our Lord?" This attitude was nonexistent. Instead,

> At the sound of Mary's greeting, Elizabeth's child leaped within her, and Elizabeth was filled with the Holy Spirit. Elizabeth gave a glad cry and exclaimed to Mary, "God has blessed you above all women, and your child is blessed. Why am I so honored, that the mother of my Lord should visit me? When I heard your greeting, the baby in my womb jumped for joy."
>
> Luke 1:41–44 NLT

Elizabeth possessed an attitude of utter humility and unspeakable joy at Mary's superior status. What a wonderful example of a woman relishing the God-given assignment of her sister-friend. Not one hint of jealousy or covetousness. She accepted their mutual roles given by God, calling it an honor for Mary to visit her. Elizabeth honored whom God honored. She didn't hesitate to affirm to Mary that she was blessed by God. Can you do that? Bless the person that God is blessing big-time? Be genuinely happy for her because she is your sister in Christ and you delight in God's abundance in her life? See no need to compare your situation or wonder why it's happening to her and not to you? Mary Slessor, a missionary to Nigeria in the 1800s, said, "Blessed the man and woman who is able to serve cheerfully in the second rank—a big test."

I love Elizabeth's example and think of it often as I pray for this same attitude of acceptance and affirmation. Regularly I pray a prayer like this:

> *Lord, help me to be genuinely happy and full of joy when you bless another woman with something I've been praying for. I want to build her up and not tear her down. I want to affirm you at work in her life. I don't want one ounce of cattiness, envy, or jealousy in my heart or gossip on my lips. I am at peace with the position and place you've given me. You know what I can handle. I don't want anything you don't want me to have.*

Praying this prayer for years has transformed my heart. I am not in competition with any woman. I can applaud her success without saying, "Lord, why not me?" I also pray this prayer of relinquishment by martyred missionary Betty Scott Stam:

> *Lord, I give up all my own plans and purposes, all my own desires and hopes, and accept thy will for my life. I give myself, my life, my all, utterly to thee to be thine forever. Fill me and seal me with thy Holy Spirit. Use me as thou wilt, send me where thou wilt, and work out thy whole will in my life at any cost, now and forever.*

When the attitudes of envy and covetousness are lurking around, it's not a pretty sight. You can tell when someone is not genuinely happy for your success. You learn to share your confidences with only Elizabeth-like friends. I believe that Mary ran to Elizabeth to share her unbelievable news because she knew she would genuinely share her joy.

People appreciate those who are flexible. It's viewed as an admirable quality and can serve to make you the stand-out person on the team!

Be Accountable

Are you accountable to anyone? Wise, godly friends can see your blind spots, but you must give them permission to "speak the truth in love" (see Ephesians 4:15). They can point out what's lying dormant in your life that should be cultivated, or the weeds that need to be extracted. No matter how nicely it is put, the truth can hurt, especially the truth about ourselves. That's why we prefer to keep as close friends those who affirm us. But as my friend Dr. Johnny Parker says, "We need to surround ourselves with friends who love us, but who are not impressed by us."

It's so easy to live in a silo, with your smartphone, tablet, and Facebook friends consuming your world. It's less threatening to communicate superficially than to take the time to build solid relationships based on trust. More Christians are finding it attractive to watch Sunday services on the Internet rather than drive a few miles to be in community with like-minded believers. Where's the accountability? If you're facing a crisis or need sound advice, who do you call?

I've had friends and relatives lovingly tell me it wasn't the right time to walk away from a job; it was the right time to end a relationship; I should prayerfully consider dropping some charges; I was selling myself short; or I was wrong in how I handled a disagreement. "Wounds from a friend can be trusted"

(Proverbs 27:6). Make sure you are accountable to someone who prizes confidentiality and whose judgment you respect. Not every person is wise or discreet.

If you are discouraged and floundering in your faith or career, that's a great time to open up to your accountability partner. Let this person or group know you want to be accountable to them about how you spend your time, what you do on a date, what you look at online, how you spend your money, or what you do to accomplish your goals. God never meant for us to face our storms and fears alone. We need someone who is not in the crisis and thinking clearly to offer support and guidance.

God never meant for us to face our storms and fears alone.

I am so thankful that when I went through the greatest crisis of my life, I had a group of three people that I talked with almost daily. I could cry, vent, and give them the latest updates. They prayed with me, comforted me, and provided perspective beyond the turbulence. I remember my mother saying to me once, "Cheryl, you want to make sure when this is all over that you conducted yourself in a way that pleased God."

I needed the accountability to shift my attitude and put the focus back where it belonged: trusting, honoring, and pleasing God.

Do you want to go to the next level in your own personal development? Home in on a candidate to be your accountability partner (preferably of the same gender and not your best friend—it could strain the relationship). Be honest about the areas about which you'd like her to ask you the hard questions. Have a consistent time for accountability. Be committed to the process. You may have to tweak it until it works for you and you see the desired results.

It's encouraging to remember that God is committed to helping us overcome any deficiencies that could potentially derail us from fulfilling His purposes. We are all flawed, but the good news is our flaws will not disqualify us from being distinct for His glory. If it's a recurring sin we're dealing with, we must be diligent to root it out (by the power of the Holy Spirit) and never settle for accepting it. Since we're all struggling in at least one area, be committed to getting a partner to help you break free and be distinctively you!

becoming distinctly you

1. Where do you need an attitude adjustment?
2. Is being flexible easy or a challenge for you? Why?
3. Name some instances where you need to practice flexibility and grace.
4. What can you learn from Elizabeth's example of accepting her God-given role?
5. Why is accountability important? List your accountability partner(s).
6. If you are not accountable to anyone, list those you will prayerfully approach about establishing an accountability partnership.

~~~ *Nugget* ~~~

Name those women in your sphere whom God is blessing big-time and whom you secretly compete with. Now pray a blessing over their lives. Ask God to expand their territory for His glory. Ask God to make you genuinely happy for their success and to make you content to play second fiddle (if that's His will). Pray that you will serve Him faithfully in your God-appointed assignment, whether it's in obscurity or on a grand stage.

19

Soul Fitness

If you want to be distinct, you must be well built. This is something you can be no matter your age, shape, or size. When I say "well built," I'm not referring to your figure due to the hours you've spent sculpting your body. I'm talking about being well built *internally*. Millions of Americans faithfully work out for hours each week. There is nothing wrong with a lifestyle of consistent exercise. The regimen is admirable. But Paul told Timothy, his young protégé, that while bodily exercise offers some value, our first priority must be spiritual strength training, developing the disciplines that strengthen the inner person, what we *don't* see. He put it this way in 1 Timothy 4:7–8: "Train yourself to be godly. For physical training is of some value, but godliness has value for all things, holding promise for both the present life and the life to come."

We become well built when we are relentless and unapologetic about doing life His way. Jesus said in Luke 6:47–48,

As for everyone who comes to me and hears my words and puts them into practice, I will show you what they are like. They are like a man building a house, who dug down deep and laid the foundation on rock. When a flood came, the torrent struck that house but could not shake it, because it was well built.

The sturdiness and depth of the foundation are must-haves for a well-built building. Show me a well-built woman, one who can weather the storms and hurricanes of life, the disappointments and rejections, and I say check out *her* foundation, the Solid Rock called Christ, and the depth of that relationship.

We become well built when we are relentless and unapologetic about doing life His way.

Months before my mate left, I began to regularly pray a prayer I don't remember praying before: "Lord, let me build my house upon a rock, so when the storms of life come, I will still be standing." I would ask myself, "Why is it I keep praying this way? What does it mean?" I found out soon enough. It was my soul anchor that kept me grounded through the ordeal; otherwise, I would have been swept away. I now understand the sense of hopelessness and despair that many women experience when life deals them an unexpected blow. I remember the words from my favorite hymn, "My Hope Is Built on Nothing Less": "On Christ, the solid rock, I stand; all other ground is sinking sand."[1] That's my story.

I learned soul fitness from my personal trainer, my mother. I've watched her pray about everything all my life. She prays in the morning, midday, and at night. She conducts prayer meetings in churches and on the phone. She loves talking to God. She influenced my father to deepen his walk with the Lord. He became a praying force. When I was growing up, it was not unusual to see my father prostrate before God in the middle of the night when I made a trip to the bathroom. They taught their eight children how to pray. If we were sick, the first person we called was Dr. Jesus. We didn't have health insurance. My oldest brother tells the story of when he was in elementary school and had to complete a form that asked for the name of his primary physician. He wrote: Dr. Jesus. The teacher called him to her desk to inquire about his answer. He said, "My mother told me that Jesus is our doctor." He was. We never made a trip to the hospital.

My mother and I logged many hours praying about which college I should attend. We only wanted God's perfect choice for me. After I was accepted into Northwestern University, we continued to pray. We wanted to be absolutely sure. The Lord finally gave us the inner confirmation we were seeking. Northwestern was His choice. I looked forward to starting college life. When I arrived on campus (sight unseen), I felt right at home. I was hundreds of miles away from home, but I knew NU was the college God ordained for me.

I told the Lord that it was important for me to continue to grow spiritually as well as intellectually. I had heard of so many students losing their spiritual way once they went to college. I didn't want to be part of that statistic. I prayed for a great Bible-teaching church. That Saturday night, after I said good-bye to my parents, I looked in the phone book for a church. I called one and it was having a special service that evening. One of the members picked me up. My first night in college I spent attending a church service. Faith Temple became my church home.

The pastor, Elder Carlis Moody, had a sterling reputation as a godly leader and great Bible teacher. The members expressed love to me and became my extended family. Once again, God had ordered my steps because of prayer.

I have never seen my mother engage in a physical workout session, but I have seen her spend many hours on her knees. Because of this regimen, God has given her incredible wisdom and insight. I remember I was excited about applying for a job that would allow me to work with a news anchor I admired. I asked my mother to pray with me for favor. A day or so later she called me and said, "The Lord told me to tell you that job is not what you think it is. It is not for you." I decided not to apply for that position, but another one became available that I did get. I got a chance to work with this anchor on another level without her being my supervisor. In just a short time I realized my mother was right. I was thanking God I did not get the job I thought I wanted. My mother loves to say, "The Holy Ghost is the Holy Ghost." His job is to lead and guide us into all truth. He is no respecter of persons. "But when he, the Spirit of truth, comes, he will guide you into all the truth. He will not speak on his own; he will speak only what he hears" (John 16:13).

Practicing soul fitness is not popular. We are encouraged to get in touch with our desires and pursue our own happiness at any cost. After all, we deserve it. We can easily become contaminated with this way of thinking. Praying and obeying the Word of God is our reality check of what is really important and what will count for eternity.

But don't just listen to God's word. You must do what it says. Otherwise, you are only fooling yourselves. For if you listen to the word and don't obey, it is like glancing at your face in a mirror. You see yourself, walk away, and forget what you look like. But if you look carefully into the perfect law that sets you free, and if you do what it says and don't forget what you heard, then God will bless you for doing it.

James 1:22–25 NLT

If you want to endure *anything* life brings your way, decide in advance (before the storm) that it's God's way or no way. Resilience will come from exercising your obedience muscle in everyday decisions.

Sometimes we may wonder if it's worth it to do life God's way, denying ourselves what appears to be a delicious pleasure. I can vouch for the fact that it pays huge dividends to serve God and have a rock-solid faith. Hebrews 11:6 says, "It is impossible to please God without faith. Anyone who wants to come to him must believe that God exists and that he rewards those who sincerely seek him" (NLT). When you have been faithfully training yourself to be godly, to be a well-built woman, faith says, "No matter what it looks like, God will see me through. There is good in the package I did not want. I don't see it today, but I see it through the eyes of faith. I have been knocked down, but I'm not out. My foundation is still standing!"

I encourage you to make spiritual fitness a priority. It doesn't matter if you started working out and then quit. Get back in the soul fitness gym. There is no membership fee. Take one day at a time. Take small steps to getting back in shape. Start with committing a few minutes a day to prayer and reading your Bible. Build on that. We can all engage in soul fitness so we will have sturdy foundations and staying power when the hurricanes of life hit us. We will be well built and ready for whatever comes our way.

becoming distinctly
you

1. How important is soul fitness to you?

2. What are you doing to stay in shape for life's obstacle courses?

3. What are your barriers to engaging in regular strength training for godliness?

4. How can you make spiritual fitness a priority, starting where you are?

5. Resilience comes from exercising the "obedience" muscle in everyday decisions. How are you doing?

20

Designer Wardrobe

What we wear and how we wear it makes a statement. I can tell a lot about a woman based on how she walks, talks, and dresses, and by her demeanor. We are in a distinct class. We represent the King of Kings. We are His ambassadors in our spheres of influence. We are royalty because we are His daughters, and that makes us princesses. There is a royal wardrobe that is fitting for us given our status. We clothe ourselves inwardly before dressing outwardly. I love what my friend Dr. Johnny Parker says: "The outer attracts, but it's the inner that impacts." This inner wardrobe is what makes us distinct.

There are ten pieces that never go out of style that we should put on daily before we leave the house. The garments are listed in Colossians 3:12–15 (NLT):

> Since God chose you to be the holy people he loves, you must
> clothe yourselves with tenderhearted mercy, kindness, humility,

gentleness, and patience. Make allowance for each other's faults, and forgive anyone who offends you. Remember, the Lord forgave you, so you must forgive others. Above all, clothe yourselves with love, which binds us all together in perfect harmony. And let the peace that comes from Christ rule in your hearts. For as members of one body you are called to live in peace. And always be thankful.

God will accept no excuses if we do not wear these articles of clothing as His daughters. They are free, but we must choose to wear them.

You may have a closet or two full of clothes. But they only get worn when you choose an outfit and put it on. We must be just as intentional about putting on all ten foundational pieces every day: tenderhearted mercy (or compassion), kindness, humility, gentleness, patience, accepting faults, forgiveness, love, peace, and thankfulness. Don't leave home without your foundation!

You may find it helpful to recite this list each morning as a prayer and say,

Lord, I don't know what I'll encounter today, but help me to be compassionate like you, not judgmental. I want to be known as a kind and caring woman. I want my thoughts to be kind, my talk to be kind, and my actions to be kind. Help me to think the best and not the worst of others. Lord, help me to have the proper estimate of myself and my abilities, and not think higher of myself than I should. I desire a true spirit of humility. I know you hate pride, even a proud look. Let me esteem my co-workers and their abilities. Don't let me name-drop, seek to impress, or toot my own horn today. You said in

Proverbs 27:2, "Let someone else praise you, and not your own mouth; an outsider, and not your own lips." I want to honor that today. May I cultivate gentleness and model mild and amiable behavior. I desire to speak gently, not rudely to people. Help me to be patient, especially with other drivers. I choose (in advance) to make allowances for others' faults, because they must bear with mine. Help me to accept others as they are without belittling them in my thoughts or with my tongue. You have so graciously forgiven me of all my sins. I want to, in turn, forgive those who have wronged me and not hold grudges and become "historical." Help me to walk in love today, sincere love. Lord, let your love flow through me in a supernatural way. May I experience your peace throughout the day, no matter what turmoil I encounter, and then please give me a great attitude of gratitude, full of thanks for all you've done for me and what you're going to do in the future.

If being clothed with these ten traits is not intentional and a priority for me, they are missing when I interact with others. Think about it. The world is consumed with how we look externally. Many of us are preoccupied with outward beauty. Billions of dollars are spent yearly on beauty products. Many promise to slow the aging process. More and more women are electing to have cosmetic surgery procedures. We all want to be beautiful, but Proverbs 31:30 says, "Charm is deceptive, and beauty is fleeting; but a woman who fears the Lord is to be praised." That's putting first things first. A distinct woman is in awe of God, possessing an overwhelming feeling of reverence and admiration produced by that which is grand, sublime, and extremely powerful. She respects His power. She takes what He says seriously. She makes a deliberate decision to focus more on her heart than on her hairstyle.

When Proverbs 31 describes God's ideal woman, nothing is said about her physical beauty. We are told that she is trustworthy and enriches her husband's life by helping, never hindering him. She's a hard worker and a great planner; she's energetic and resourceful, a woman of strength and dignity. She's wise, considerate of the poor, and dresses impeccably. Kindness is the rule for everything she says.

When Proverbs 31 describes God's ideal woman, nothing is said about her physical beauty.

God considers a woman dressed with these attributes extremely valuable. She is rare. Her price? Worth more than precious rubies. I call her a distinct woman. She is a model we can all follow because these are inward attributes that flow outward. We can possess them with practice, desire, and diligence.

In the New Testament, Peter emphasizes inner beauty when he tells women:

> Your beauty should not come from outward adornment, such as elaborate hairstyles and the wearing of gold jewelry or fine clothes. Rather, it should be that of your inner self, the unfading beauty of a gentle and quiet spirit, which is of great worth in God's sight.
>
> 1 Peter 3:3–4

What is meant by a "gentle and quiet spirit"? A gentle or meek woman is poised with strength under control. The Master controls her power. For example, this woman has the vocabulary to tell others off and give them a piece of her mind (in Jesus' name), but she refuses to do so. "The Greek word for *meek* was commonly used to describe wild animals that had been domesticated—trained, tamed, and otherwise harnessed. . . . Once broken, this animal does not require much correction. He has learned to accept the reins of his master, and a gentle tug is all that is needed to urge him one direction or the other."[1]

A woman who has placed the reins of her life in the guiding hand of the Master gives up control. She is humble and gentle and shows patience with others and herself. She is teachable, is open for correction, and possesses a willingness to be instructed. She is not a know-it-all and does not think or say, "Who does she think she is to tell *me* this!"

A woman with a calm (quiet) spirit is not easily vexed. She remains calm despite her circumstances, because she trusts God. This doesn't mean she never talks. It means her spirit is calm. She is not fearful of her future, not agitated. Why? Her hope and trust are in a God who always does what is right and just.

When you have a designer wardrobe, instead of being a three-C woman (comparing, competing, and coveting), you focus on becoming a three-D woman poised with discretion, discernment, and diligence. Discretion is the quality of displaying caution and self-restraint, handling practical matters judiciously, managing carefully. This woman knows what to say, when to say it, how much to say, and to whom. "Discretion will protect you, and understanding will guard you" (Proverbs 2:11).

Discernment is being perceptive, showing insight and judgment. "The discerning heart seeks knowledge" (Proverbs 15:14). A discerning woman is careful about what she feeds her mind, the books she reads, the movies and television shows she watches. "The heart of the discerning acquires knowledge" (Proverbs 18:15).

Diligence is marked by persevering, painstaking effort. "Diligent hands will rule" (Proverbs 12:24). "The desires of the diligent are fully satisfied" (Proverbs 13:4). The diligent are excellent planners with a stick-to-it mentality, and it pays off in huge dividends. "The plans of the diligent lead to profit as surely as haste leads to poverty" (Proverbs 21:5).

How would someone describe your wardrobe? Do you win people with your physical or godly attributes? By your looks, or your love for God? Would they say you are kind, loving, humble, and discreet? A distinct woman will own a designer wardrobe that never goes out of style.

becoming distinctly
you

1. Read Colossians 3:12–15. Which of the ten pieces of clothing have you *not* been wearing?

2. Read Proverbs 31:10–31. Which attributes do you most admire? Why?

3. Why should your priority be on your internal rather than external appearance?

4. What is a three-D woman? How can you cultivate these
attractive attributes?

~~~ *Nugget* ~~~

Make it part of your daily regimen to declare that you are putting on the ten garments listed in Colossians 3. Strive to never
leave home without them.

21

Prizing Wisdom

Society prizes knowledge and being smart. It's nice to have people call you smart, but being distinct requires wisdom. Knowledge or being smart is having the facts. Wisdom is skillfully applying those facts to life. A distinct woman esteems wisdom above knowledge.

How many "smart," influential people have done dumb things? Regularly in the news there are stories of smart, affluent, powerful people accused of doing or saying something that indicates they may be *smart* but not *wise*.

If you're like me, you have done or said something that was not wise. Because we have all blown it in some way or another, it should make us more merciful in our judgments of others' failures and foibles. We should seek to learn from their mistakes so we don't repeat them. We all need a big dose of wisdom. God considered getting wisdom so crucial that one entire book of the Bible is devoted to it: Proverbs.

Don't turn your back on wisdom, for she will protect you. Love her, and she will guard you. Getting wisdom is the wisest thing you can do! And whatever else you do, develop good judgment. If you prize wisdom, she will make you great. Embrace her, and she will honor you. She will place a lovely wreath on your head; she will present you with a beautiful crown.

Proverbs 4:6–9 NLT

How do you esteem wisdom? Proverbs 2:2 says, "Tune your ears to wisdom, and concentrate on understanding" (NLT). We are to consult God first about everything because He personifies wisdom. We are bombarded with so many voices, so many avenues for advice: talk show hosts, success gurus, the latest tabloid or magazine article, celebrities, the Internet. If we want to be wise, these voices must be faint or secondary. The primary frequency we should be tuned to is what God says in His Word on any and every matter: our finances, our definition of beauty, success, singleness, marriage, career, and family.

Proverbs 2 uses such words as *cry out, call out, look for, search,* and *seek* when it comes to wisdom. Esteeming wisdom is not saying a one-minute prayer when you have an emergency. It is a lifelong pursuit. "For the Lord gives wisdom; from his mouth come knowledge and understanding" (Proverbs 2:6).

It's okay to say, "Lord, I don't know what to do, but you do. Is this a good deal?" It's fine to say, "Lord, I think I know what to do, but I still need to check with you before moving ahead. Is this the house you want me to buy? Is this the person you want me to marry?" I strongly suggest not making a move until you have clearly heard from God. I've regretted every time I did not do so. "In their hearts humans plan their course, but the Lord establishes their steps" (Proverbs 16:9).

Wisdom is available to every person just for the asking. James, the half brother of Jesus, wrote:

> If you need wisdom, ask our generous God, and he will give it to you. He will not rebuke you for asking. But when you ask him, be sure that your faith is in God alone. Do not waver, for a person with divided loyalty is as unsettled as a wave of the sea that is blown and tossed by the wind. Such people should not expect to receive anything from the Lord. Their loyalty is divided between God and the world, and they are unstable in everything they do.
>
> James 1:5–8 NLT

James gives us a guarantee that if we really want God's perspective on any decision we need to make, all we have to do is ask Him and believe that He will tell us, and He will. God wants us to make the best decision more than we do. He never tires of our coming to Him for advice. But what do most of us do? We ask our family members, our girlfriends, our life coaches, what they think we should do. Unfortunately, God is not on the list, and if He is, He's at the bottom. We should go to God first and wait patiently for the answer in His time. But equally important is to rid ourselves of our strong desires and self-will while we wait. The dominating force in our decisions must be the will of God. If we are at that point in our soul, in our gut, we can hear the voice of God. If not, there will be major fog, a blockage.

The dominating force in our decisions must be the will of God.

I've discovered that much of my prayer time is needed to get me out of the way, to change the focus of my prayers and fantasies from what I want to what God knows is best. So many times we think God is too slow, that He's holding up the answer that we need on purpose, when in reality, we are not open to His will because we have been praying our own agenda. I've done this so many times. Here's an example.

When I finally believed that it was the right time to apply to graduate school, I decided that I would only apply to one: Columbia University in New York City. Because of a broken heart, I wanted to leave the Chicago area, so I was not going to apply to my alma mater, Northwestern, even though its school of journalism (like Columbia's) was considered one of the top programs in the nation. I convinced myself that I needed a fresh start.

A writing test was required as part of Columbia's admissions process. I could take it in the presence of one of its alums in the Chicago area. As it turned out, one of the professors at Northwestern's journalism program was an alumnus, so I agreed to meet him on campus to take the test. Afterward he said casually, "Why don't you also apply to Northwestern's program?" For the first time I was open to the idea. I decided to apply (with NU being my backup).

I said to the Lord, "Lord, please let me get admitted to only one school so I will not be confused and I'll know clearly where you'd like me to go." I was admitted to both. I was confused. I began polling mentors, colleagues, friends, and family members. It was a toss-up. My mother believed God wanted me to return to Northwestern. I didn't want to hear that, so I ignored that option.

Finally the deadline was approaching to make a choice. I had decided that Columbia was best for me (for selfish reasons). I had not been open to an alternative. That's why I was not experiencing the peace of God that comes with His answers. I decided to get down to business with my praying. I went in my room, shut the door, and sat in the middle of the bed. I may have been heartbroken, but I did want to obey God's heart more than mine. I confessed to the Lord my sin of wanting my own way and assuming that Columbia was His choice. I admitted that I thought leaving the area was the best way for me to mend my broken heart. Then I said, "Lord, I want your will more than anything else. I will gladly attend the school that you know is best for me. Just make your will clear to me in a way that I will understand." I remained still and my spirit quiet. I was expectantly waiting for God to answer. In just a few minutes, the peace of God swept over my soul. The confusion ceased. I had His answer without a doubt: Northwestern. I never questioned it again.

I am so glad I took the necessary time to get God's viewpoint on this major decision that would determine the future course of my life. I became a candidate for the NBC News program as a result of attending NU.

I find it extremely helpful in my development to have an example or model of what I'm hoping to be, a woman who esteems wisdom. That example for me is Abigail. Her story is told in 1 Samuel 25. She is the only woman in the Bible described as wise. While she was wise, her husband, Nabal, had a reputation for being a fool. Nabal not only did foolish things, but also his name meant "fool." He was very wealthy, which also goes to show that having a lot of money does not necessarily mean you are a wise person.

David had done a good deed for Nabal, protecting his supplies and workforce of shepherds around the clock when they were in the field. David asked Nabal to treat his workers with kindness. After all, one good turn deserves another. But not according to Nabal. David wanted him to feed his six hundred men. Nabal had a short memory, and insulted David by saying, "Who are you and why should I take my bread, water, and meat that I have slaughtered for my crew and give it to yours? I don't know these guys" (see vv. 10–11).

David was livid. He told four hundred of his men to get their swords because they had some business to take care of; no more kindness to Nabal, if that's the thanks he got for his good deed.

In the meantime, one of Nabal's servants told Abigail all about it, how David was gracious and Nabal was not, and now their lives were in jeopardy as a result of Nabal's foolish decision to treat David rudely. Abigail's life was also at stake because of her husband's rash decision. What did she do? She could not control what her husband did in a fit of rage. She knew him and his temper. So she did what she could. She was a wise woman with the ability to think on her feet. She knew that time was not on her side. She acted quickly. Sometimes we have just a small window of opportunity to make a difference. She organized a huge care package for David and his men. She apparently knew the proverb that says a gift pacifies anger. It's hard to be angry with someone who showers you with gifts. Maybe she also knew that the way to a man's heart is through his stomach.

Abigail approached David on a donkey. He had just been recounting how Nabal had treated him and promised to kill Nabal and his whole family. Abigail respected his authority by her actions and attitude. She bowed before David, showing honor and humility. She called him *lord*. She knew he was the future king of Israel.

Do you respect God-given authority because it's the right thing to do and it honors God? You may disagree with the person's actions, attitudes, or political persuasion, but do you respect the authority of his position, whether it's your boss or your husband? That's wisdom. Abigail could have approached David with indignation; after all, he was threatening to wipe out her entire family and workforce. But no, she had a spirit of humility. She called David her master, herself his servant. She asked for permission to speak.

Abigail's wisdom led her to be loyal to her husband. She could have done nothing, saying, "This man is a fool. He deserves to die. Good riddance. I'll just pray that God takes care of me when David comes." Instead, she explained to David that Nabal was just a foolish man and he should not take his actions personally. He was just living up to his name. She was not disrespectful of Nabal, just acknowledging how he was. It was his nature to act rashly and foolishly.

Abigail modeled discretion and discernment. She knew it was best not to tell Nabal what she was doing initially. She was discerning in her approach with David. She knew how to calm him. She didn't tell him *not* to kill her husband. Instead, she gave him reasons why he wouldn't want to do that: David had been anointed to be king and he wouldn't want blood on his hands when he took the throne. God was able to take care of his enemies. She realized that sometimes when we have been offended, we lose sight of the big picture and try to take our battles into our own hands. She asked him to forgive Nabal, saying the Lord would certainly make a lasting dynasty for David because he fought the Lord's battles, and He would take care of David's enemies. There would be no need for David to have a guilty conscience. "Calmness can lay great offenses to rest" (Ecclesiastes 10:4). What a wise, discerning, discreet woman.

David praised her for her wise judgment. He acknowledged that she was a godsend, keeping him from avenging his enemies. He told her in 1 Samuel 25:34, "If you had not come quickly to meet me, not one male belonging to Nabal would have been left alive by daybreak." David told her to go home in peace because he had heard her words and granted her request. Mission accomplished. She saved her household.

What happened next? She went back home. Her husband was having a party and was very drunk. Discretion told her this was not the right time to tell him what she had done. She did so the next morning when he was sober. He had a heart attack, and ten days later, verse 38 says, "The Lord struck Nabal and he died." Abigail didn't have to do a thing. Neither did David. "It is mine to avenge; I will repay, says the Lord" (Romans 12:19). When David learned of Nabal's death, he gave praise to God for upholding his cause. He also knew a wise, good woman when he met one. He sent for Abigail, asking her to be his wife.

Pursuing wisdom will make you distinct.

What was her response? Once again she possessed a spirit of humility and servanthood. She said, "I am your servant and am ready to serve you and wash the feet of my lord's servants" (1 Samuel 25:41). Yes, Abigail was a wise and beautiful woman, but she also possessed a spirit of serving others, from the lowest to the greatest. I believe that spirit made her more attractive than her physical beauty.

Pursuing wisdom will make you distinct. Why not start with reading one chapter a day in Proverbs. There are 31. It's my goal to do this every month. It takes less than five minutes a day.

Joyful is the person who finds wisdom, and the one who gains understanding. For wisdom is more profitable than silver, and her wages are better than gold. Wisdom is more precious than rubies; nothing you desire can compare with her. She offers you long life in your right hand, and riches and honor in her left. She will guide you down delightful paths; all her ways are satisfying. Wisdom is a tree of life to those who embrace her; happy are those who hold her tightly.

Proverbs 3:13–18 NLT

becoming distinctly
you

1. What's the difference between knowledge and wisdom?
2. What does it take to develop the habit of seeking God's wisdom?
3. List the wise attributes Abigail possessed.
4. How committed are you to pursuing and prizing wisdom?

~~ Nugget ~~

Make a commitment for the rest of your life to read the chapter of Proverbs that corresponds to each day. Purpose also to apply the wisdom principles. If you miss a day, start again the next.

22

Count the Cost

Being distinct has a price tag: due diligence. Are you willing to pay the price? It requires doing what we can do and confidently expecting God to do what we cannot do. Preparation is key. "Wise choices will watch over you. Understanding will keep you safe" (Proverbs 2:11 NLT).

I have never regretted moving too slowly when making a major decision, but I have regretted making a quick decision without completing the fact-gathering process. My mother gave me this advice when I was a teenager: "Take the time to count up the cost before you do anything. Think through the consequences of your actions." The "thinking through" part can take a while. We live in a microwave society that urges, "Do it now." I've learned the hard way that it's always best to wait. We can make our choices, but we can't choose the consequences of those choices.

It's a great feeling when you are pleased with the choice you've made. When I know the pros and cons beforehand, I am making an informed decision and am willing to live with it. Over the years I have never regretted where I chose to live or the car I bought because I did my due diligence and made the decision that was right for me at the time. I made sure I was not biting off more than I could chew or acting impetuously. We all have our own way of processing information. It's important to always be true to it. I have friends who move much faster than I do on a deal or opportunity. When I've tried to speed up to their level, I've fumbled and was uncomfortable because they were moving too fast for my comfort level. It worked for them, but not for me. This is part of being authentically me. I now realize that I will not miss an opportunity if my God-given speed is a turtle's pace. When I've needed to speed it up, I received the unction and grace to do so. Be true to who you are as you prepare and plan.

Jesus said,

> Suppose one of you wants to build a tower. Won't you first sit down and estimate the cost to see if you have enough money to complete it? For if you lay the foundation and are not able to finish it, everyone who sees it will ridicule you, saying, "This person began to build and wasn't able to finish."

> Luke 14:28–30

I see God at work when I'm pondering possible options. He uses the process of investigation and prayer to get me to His desired result. After working at the Christian television station in Chicago for a couple of years as an assistant producer of a daily talk show, I had a strong desire to pursue a job in broadcast news. As I thought about it, the idea came to pursue a graduate degree in journalism at a top university first before job hunting. I believed this avenue would provide me skills and credibility as a solid candidate for a position in news. That was the right course for me. I have never regretted that decision, but it is not for everyone. I have friends who got great jobs in television news without a bachelor's degree in journalism. Their careers soared. It's an individual decision. But we can count on God's leading when we do our part and then He steps in to do His.

King David's heart's desire was to build a magnificent temple for God. He made elaborate plans to build it. But God told him he was not to do so because he was a warrior. David didn't let the plans lie dormant. He gave them to his son Solomon, the next king of Israel. They were extensive. He told Solomon to be strong and to do the work.

> Then David gave his son Solomon the plans for the portico of the temple, its buildings, its storerooms, its upper parts, its inner rooms. . . . He gave him the plans of all that the Spirit had put in his mind for the courts of the temple of the Lord and all the surrounding rooms, for the treasuries of the temple of God and for the treasuries for the dedicated things.
>
> 1 Chronicles 28:11–12

God was intimately involved with placing His detailed plans in David's heart. He will do the same for us as we chart our distinct course.

This is how Daniel and his three friends lived. They refused to compromise God's principles. As a result, Daniel was thrown into a lions' den, his friends bound and thrown into a fiery furnace. They would rather die than disobey God. The outcome of their obedience didn't matter. That was God's business; theirs was to obey.

Daniel's friends survived the piping hot furnace: "The fire had not harmed their bodies, nor was a hair of their heads singed;

their robes were not scorched, and there was no smell of fire on them" (Daniel 3:27). The king started praising their God after this show of His power. Nebuchadnezzar said,

> Praise be to the God of Shadrach, Meshach and Abednego, who has sent his angel and rescued his servants! They trusted in him and defied the king's command and were willing to give up their lives rather than serve or worship any god except their own God. . . . No other god can save in this way.
>
> Daniel 3:28–29

Then the king promoted them.

Daniel had a similar distinctive outcome. "And when Daniel was lifted from the den, no wound was found on him, because he had trusted in his God" (Daniel 6:23). The king was so astounded by God's power that he issued a decree that all the people must fear and reverence Daniel's God. And like his friends, Daniel prospered during the reign of the king.

God is waiting on us to get serious about serving Him wholeheartedly.

That same God is our God, who is waiting on us to get serious about serving Him wholeheartedly. We will then see His power on display in our lives. "For the eyes of the Lord range throughout the earth to strengthen those who hearts are fully committed to him" (2 Chronicles 16:9).

Decide to be that woman who prepares for her destiny by counting up the cost and making ample preparation to be distinct.

becoming distinctly
you

1. Are you willing to pay the cost to be distinctly you?
2. Name the preparation necessary to be distinctly you—the student, single, wife, mother, or career professional.
3. What is your process for making good decisions?
4. Read Daniel 3 and 6. What were the "to-die-for" convictions of these friends? What was the outcome?
5. What are your convictions to live by?

—— *Nugget* ——

Read again 2 Chronicles 16:9. Is your heart fully committed to God? If not, decide today to be in this distinct class. Pray this prayer:

Lord, I admit that I've been holding back. I have not given you my whole heart. I'm sorry about this. I am now ready to entrust to you my whole heart, my whole being. I am ready to be fully committed to you and your distinct plan for my life. You are the true and living God who can be trusted 100 percent. My heart is yours.

23

Live in the Now

I have always struggled to be fully present in the now. When I was in high school, I was daydreaming about college. When I was in college, I fantasized about transferring to another college or applying to business school for early admission. Once I got a job in television, it wasn't long before I was thinking about the next move. I don't recommend this habit. I've worked hard to break it because it robs you of enjoying where you are and the lessons God wants you to learn. There is a reason for each season. It typically prepares you for the next and helps to develop your skills and character for a future assignment. That's why it's important not to miss or disregard a step.

I've been constantly amazed at how one job always prepares me for the next. After leaving the NBC-owned television station, I took a contract assignment with a small PBS station in Washington to write, report, and produce a one-hour special. I'd never thought about being a documentary producer. Once

I began focusing on the project and doing my research, I found that I absolutely loved it. I was thriving. I was more suited to doing this than being a daily general assignment reporter. It fit with how my brain works and with my inclination toward details. I enjoyed immersing myself in one topic for weeks and watching the concept materialize into an hour-long program. I would not have known this if the door had not closed at the other station.

I decided to embrace this new experience and learn from my past. As a result of the success of the first special, I was asked to stay on to produce another documentary that won a Silver Award from the Corporation of Public Broadcasting. While at the station, I enrolled in a mini-program in Boston that enhanced my skills as a producer. I interacted with and learned from top writers and producers of documentaries that aired on PBS. I was eligible for the program because I worked at a PBS affiliate. It was enriching and invaluable in improving my skills.

I always had an interest in anchoring but never had the opportunity. I noticed that Maryland Public Television aired news briefs throughout its evening programming. I contacted the executive producer and found out MPT hired freelancers to fill in for the permanent anchor when needed. He was willing to give me a chance. It wasn't long before I was filling in regularly. I loved anchoring and was a natural. It was another strength I didn't know I had.

When you live in the now, you are open to possibilities that expand your reach. I never dreamed of being a producer when I was in graduate school. I never thought about it. I wasn't sure if my dream of being an anchor or program host would ever materialize. But while you're waiting, don't be afraid to take advantage of an opportunity that will get you out of your comfort zone. When I applied for the on-air position with BET News, management was looking for someone who could do it all: report, produce, write, and anchor. All my previous jobs made me an attractive candidate. I didn't understand my career path then. It was different from other colleagues', but it was perfect for preparing me for God's unique assignment.

When you live in the now, you are open to possibilities that expand your reach.

Remember when Joseph dreamed that one day his father and brothers would bow down to him? Shortly after that vision, his life appeared to go downhill. His jealous brothers came close to killing him; instead, they put him in a pit and sold him into slavery. From his master's house he landed in prison (charged with a crime he did not commit), forgotten for years. Through it all, we never hear one complaint from Joseph about his dire circumstances, no report of suicidal depression. Instead we read in Genesis 39:2–4,

> The Lord was with Joseph so that he prospered, and he lived in the house of his Egyptian master. When his master saw that the Lord was with him and that the Lord gave him success in everything he did, Joseph found favor in his eyes and became his attendant.

While he was in prison,

> The Lord was with him; he showed him kindness and granted him favor in the eyes of the prison warden. So the warden put Joseph in charge of all those held in the prison, and he was made

responsible for all that was done there. . . . The Lord was with Joseph and gave him success in whatever he did.

Genesis 39:21–23

Joseph flourished wherever he was, making the most of every opportunity. He refused to be consumed with the thought, *This is not fair. What did I do to deserve a life like this?* He never saw himself as a victim. Wherever he was, he was all there. Martyred missionary Jim Elliot said, "Live to the hilt every situation you believe to be the will of God."

After spending more than two years in prison, Joseph got his big break on a day that started out like any other day. He thought he had been forgotten by the one released prisoner he had asked to remember him. In God's perfect timing, the chief cupbearer remembered Joseph's ability to interpret dreams, when the Pharaoh had a troubling dream that no one on his staff could interpret. Joseph was quickly brought from the dungeon to put his skill on display. Even then, Joseph refused to take the credit that only belonged to God.

> Pharaoh said to Joseph, "I had a dream, and no one can interpret it. But I have heard it said of you that when you hear a dream you can interpret it."
> "I cannot do it," Joseph replied to Pharaoh, "but God will give Pharaoh the answer he desires."

Genesis 41:15–16

Everything Joseph had experienced strategically prepared him for this moment. He interpreted the Pharaoh's dreams perfectly and offered a workable plan. The Pharaoh then selected Joseph to be next in command. Who but God could orchestrate that swift promotion and give Joseph such distinction for His glory and purposes? When the famine spread, Joseph was responsible for providing grain for his own family for their survival. Joseph, free of any anger or bitterness, was able to see God's hand in guiding his life. When we live on purpose in the now, striving for excellence in every assignment, we are saying to God, "I trust you, and I want to represent you well. This is not what I signed up for, but you don't make mistakes. There is something you want me to learn in this experience. May I glorify you while I'm learning it." It's okay to ask God what the takeaway is so you don't miss it. We can look in reverse at Joseph's dilemma and see that it was God's plan all along for him to end up in Egypt as a slave, be thrown into a prison, forgotten, and released at the opportune time so he would come to the attention of the Pharaoh and become his chief officer. That's the position God needed him in to fulfill His bigger purpose of delivering His people.

Refuse to process your life from your perspective. It won't add up. Evaluating it from God's perspective reveals a master plan that is simple, yet complex. He is the only one who knows all the parts and is able to execute them masterfully. Our job is to live in the now. He'll take care of our now, our past, and our future.

becoming distinctly you

1. How much time do you spend thinking about past mistakes or present desires? How much time and energy do you spend concentrating on where you are right now and what needs to be done today?

2. What are some possibilities available to you right now that you need to take advantage of?

3. Read the story of Joseph (Genesis 37, 39–41). Reflect on Joseph's response to his dire circumstances.

4. Genesis 39:2–3 says, "The Lord was with Joseph. . . . The Lord gave him success in everything he did." How can you prosper for the glory of God in your situation?

5. Do you really believe that everything you have experienced is preparation for your distinct path? If so, how is this belief reflected in your attitudes and actions?

24

Control *You*

Are you guilty of trying to control others, their decisions, their reactions, and their opinions of you? I am, yet there is so little we can control in the lives of others. We certainly can't control the other driver swerving while talking on his cell phone, the person choosing not to respond to an email or text, or a spouse walking out of a marriage. How many times have you gotten upset or angry about somebody else's decision that impacted you? I have many times. Then I tell myself, "I can only control *me*: my attitude, my speech, my response, and my choices."

"Control what you can control" has become one of my favorite maxims. When I remember this, my spirit returns to the setting *calm*. I am empowered by this choice. I can't stop someone from disliking me or talking about me, but I can choose to have a God-honoring response. I put the focus back where it belongs: doing what I'm called to do.

Change is happening all around us whether we like it or not. I am not the first person to embrace change. I am open to change if it's for the better, but I encounter a lot of change that's heading the opposite direction. I'm in the midst of an attitude adjustment right now. My neighborhood bank changed hands, and my favorite manager lost his job. My favorite Chinese carryout is skimping on the fortune cookies and crunchy noodles (now I get one package instead of two) and putting less chicken in my chicken fried rice. My discount dry cleaner was bought out. Prices went up, quality went down, and familiar faces are now gone. I pay more at the grocery store, but get less. What's going on? After bemoaning all this, I say once again to myself, "Control what you can control. All these things are out of your hands. But you can either accept the changes or choose another bank, carryout, and dry cleaner. You do have the power of choice."

Are you able to differentiate what you can control from what you can't control? If so, it will save you a lot of time, frustration, and needless conversation.

Don't Judge

Here are some practical ways you can control *you*. First, don't judge. We seldom have all the facts about changes. We're not in a position to know. My pastor once said, "Remember the pancake rule. There are two sides to every story." It takes great prayer, self-examination, and discipline not to judge. Jesus had some strong advice about judging:

> Do not judge others, and you will not be judged. For you will
> be treated as you treat others. The standard you use in judging

is the standard by which you will be judged. And why worry about a speck in your friend's eye when you have a log in your own? How can you think of saying to your friend, "Let me help you get rid of that speck in your eye," when you can't see past the log in your own eye? Hypocrite! First get rid of the log from your own eye; then you will see well enough to deal with the speck in your friend's eye.

Matthew 7:1–5 NLT

When I mess up, I want people to go easy on me. This passage is convicting because Jesus says I need to first be merciful toward others when they miss the mark. More and more I am choosing to pray before I speak (I need to do it even more). Just the other day I was tempted to tell a friend she should stop doing something because it was unattractive. It was on the tip of my tongue. And then I heard the small voice of the Holy Spirit say, "Don't do it." He reminded me that this was my standard—not a black-and-white issue—and it wasn't worth causing a strain in a relationship. Over time she may come to that same conclusion, He said, but if she did not, I was not to judge her. It was minor. We would still both get to heaven. This was not a deal breaker. I am so glad I kept my mouth shut.

Mind Your Own Business

Here's one of my favorite verses: "Make it your ambition to lead a quiet life: You should mind your own business and work with your hands, just as we told you" (1 Thessalonians 4:11). Apparently, this was as big an issue then as it is now, because Paul says it again in 2 Thessalonians 3:11: "We hear that some among you are idle and disruptive. They are not busy; they are busybodies." The temptation to meddle in other people's business is huge because of social media. We are privy to what's going on in their lives because of Facebook, Twitter, blogs, websites, and other social media options. You may have thousands of Facebook friends, but are they really friends? I doubt it. We're on overload because we know too much about the lives of others. We Google them because "inquiring minds want to know."

A woman who wants to be distinct will set boundaries, practice discipline, and say, "That's not really my business, so I will not inquire or give an opinion." It takes a lot of willpower, because these days everybody wants to be a pundit and deliver their opinion about any and everything. I heard author Elisabeth Elliot share many times what the Lord told her one day: "Remember, there are very few things that are really your business." Then she added, "Never pass up an opportunity to keep your mouth shut." A friend of mine, when asked about something that does not relate to him, responds, "That's not even close to my business." A distinct woman will also limit her own self-disclosure. My mother has told me often, "You don't tell *anybody* everything."

Be Likable

You can choose to be likable. It's not left up to you to be the most beautiful or the smartest, but you can control being likable. Do people genuinely like you, or is there something about your personality that causes others to be repulsed? When we are gracious, good, friendly, and kind, people will want to help us fulfill our divine destiny and be distinct.

I've said for years, "People hire who they like." If there are two candidates with equal credentials and experience, the one who is more likable will get the job. In some instances, the most friendly and warm candidate with a great attitude may be less qualified, but her winning personality will give her the edge. Why? No one wants to work with someone who is arrogant, negative, catty, difficult, rude, critical, unfriendly, or unsocial, even if they are the smartest person in the room.

It's not left up to you to be the most beautiful or the smartest, but you can control being likable.

I have talked with women who have had difficulty advancing in their jobs. They were educated, hardworking, and competent. They couldn't figure out what was holding them back. My assessment? They needed to work on being likable and more flexible.

We can't change our IQ, but we can change our LQ, our likability quotient. Proverbs 3:3–4 (NLT) says, "Never let loyalty and kindness leave you! Tie them around your neck as a reminder. Write them deep within your heart. Then you will find favor with both God and people, and you will earn a good reputation." *Miss Likability* shows up wearing kindness and loyalty, plus a beautiful smile. A smile is an instant free facelift.

Jesus, our ultimate role model, was deity in the flesh, and he was likable. People from all walks of life were drawn to Him. His loving, kind, compassionate, gracious words and demeanor were a huge part of His attraction. Jesus was always the smartest person whenever He arrived on the scene, but He never spoke in a condescending way to the poor and marginalized. He always knew what others were thinking, but He let them complete their sentences. He never made others feel small or insulted their intelligence because He was much smarter.

Most of my adult life I've been working on being more likable. I pray to be gracious, gentle, good, and giving. It takes practice to be relational if that's not your normal personality or you didn't grow up in an environment where you were taught and encouraged to be friendly.

The early years in my career I was totally focused on one thing: excellence. I arrived at work ready to work, with no time to play or fraternize. I had a job to do, and it did not include small talk. After one assignment, when the general manager praised my work, I said, "I wonder what my colleagues think about me." He answered, "I can tell you, but you don't want to know. I just know you get the job done." I smugly focused on his affirmation and decided not to probe the opinion of my peers. I revisited that later when I came face-to-face with the same reality.

I was once again working hard to do an excellent job in a new position with a new company. I didn't have time to engage in conversations with my co-workers unless they related to my assignment. While my boss was pleased with my work, I had no camaraderie with my peers. I started praying about this. I was always complaining to God about them and the work environment. One day He told me, "You need to change to bring about a change." I couldn't believe it! "You mean, Lord, *I'm* the problem?" He answered, "Yes, you're the Christian in the workplace." He pointed out that I never sought to be friendly or a bridge builder. Proverbs 18:24 says, "A man who has friends must himself be friendly" (NKJV).

Once God had my attention, I prayed specifically for ways to rectify the situation. He told me to take time to actually talk to my co-workers about their lives, their weekends. I prayed that I would show sincere interest. The Lord said, "It will take you only a few minutes each day to engage and be genuinely friendly." I began to do that intentionally and it made a huge difference. My colleagues started to get a different impression of me. The other thing I did was to invest in inexpensive but meaningful Christmas gifts for my co-workers. I bought the gifts throughout the year and saved them for the holiday. I expected nothing in return, but Proverbs 21:14 does say, "A gift in secret pacifies anger" (NKJV). Little by little I began to change their perception of me and forge relationships with co-workers because I took the initiative to become more likable.

Likability remains at the top of my prayer list. It's so easy to be me-focused rather than others-centered. Here are some practical tips for gaining ground in this area: (1) Pray regularly to find favor with others. It's God who grants it. A person will begin to like you, but you don't know why. "The king's heart is like a stream of water directed by the Lord; he guides it wherever he pleases" (Proverbs 21:1 NLT). God gave Daniel, Joseph, and Esther favor with key officials in pagan societies. Their likability was all part of God's plan for them to achieve His purposes. (2) Ask the Lord to show you *you*. Ask, "Am I causing the blockage in this relationship? What do I need to change?" (3) Develop an action plan for being more personable. It could include things like smiling more, taking an interest in others without being nosy, offering a sincere compliment, even saying "please" and "thank you." Always seek to build up others and not tear them down. (4) Practice the plan daily until it becomes second nature. (5) Find and memorize Scriptures that encourage friendliness.

No matter how likable you are, some people will refuse to like you or forgive you. This is when you remind yourself that you can only control *you*. I have experienced the pain of rejection by unforgiving friends who were Christ followers. I had to re-member this verse: "If it is possible, as far as it depends on you, live at peace with everyone" (Romans 12:18). We are human, so we will make mistakes, disappoint, and offend. We all have a choice in our response. The right one is to always do what will honor and glorify God. Leave the results to Him.

Be Confident of Your Value

An artist determines the value of his masterpiece. If I were to try to sell something that I painted, it wouldn't get a dime because I can't draw a square straight. I have no value as an artist. My name means nothing in the art world. In 1990, a painting by Van Gogh sold for a record $82.5 million. Why? It had his name on it. Ephesians 2:10 says, "We are God's masterpiece. He has created us anew in Christ Jesus, so we can do the good things he planned for us long ago" (NLT). God has determined your value. He says you are a masterpiece. That verse alone should mark us for the rest of our lives, but unfortunately, too many women give greater credence to what others call them: unworthy, unattractive, uninspired. If you believe what your Creator says about you, it will be evident by the choices you make, how you carry yourself, and what you choose to control. Catherine, the Duchess of Cambridge, is in line to be the queen of England one day because she's married to an heir of the throne, Prince William. She is already carrying herself like a future queen. She is walking in her position of royalty.

We are "a chosen people, a royal priesthood, a holy nation, God's special possession, that you may declare the praises of him who called you out of darkness into his wonderful light" (1 Peter 2:9). When we remember that we are God's masterpiece, created to do a distinct work, that we are chosen and royalty, we will carry ourselves with strength and dignity no matter where we live or what our occupation or marital status is.

People treat us the way we train them. They take their cues from us. When you conduct yourself like a lady, you are treated like one. Meditate on these questions and ask yourself: "How do I want to be perceived? How do I want men to treat me? My co-workers? My relatives?" Model that. When you value *you* because God created you, you won't sell yourself short in any area of life: career, dating, or marriage. You won't be desperate to take anything. When you know your value, it doesn't mean that others will always appreciate you or come up to your standards. Be prepared to walk away. You can't control them.

> When you value you because God created you, you won't sell yourself short in any area of life.

There have been times when men I really liked did not value me or my stand to remain sexually pure. They chose to walk away from the relationship. Was I disappointed? Yes. Did I cry? Yes. Did I have any regrets? No. Why? I value God and me more than a dream of a permanent relationship with someone who does not honor God or me. When you value yourself, you remember that some others may not.

Think about it this way. Each store has a different value system. Anybody can shop at Walmart. It's affordable. They have low prices every day; you'll see people from every walk of life there. You go for bargains and you find them. That's the Walmart brand. High-end specialty stores have a different philosophy. They don't want everybody's business. They cater to the elite. That's why the prices are out of reach for the common person. They never apologize for the price tag. If you have to ask the price, you are in the wrong store. During a recession, the prices don't go down. They know their worth. It may take a while, but their loyal customers will be back, glad to pay the price.

Since we are God's masterpieces, of royal lineage, why would we ever cheapen our market value by our actions? Let's say you're single and know that having sex before marriage is a sin. You start dating a guy and he keeps pressuring you to lower your price as if he's at a bargain basement sale. You finally consent and have sex with him. He is surprised (he may never tell you this), but takes advantage of the "moonlight special." He gets the goods and never sees you the same way again.

The flip side is that when we value ourselves and know our worth, the man who really wants us will recognize our value (above rubies) and will rise to the standard. Now, it may take a while for the right "buyer" to come along because not everyone can afford us, just like not everybody can afford what's inside the high-end specialty store. But as I love to say, you only need *one* man, the right man. This is not a popularity contest, but a quality, distinction contest. The woman who knows her value (because she is God's masterpiece) is not trying to attract every man, but a godly man, who knows her worth and will do what he has to do to win her heart.

Remember Jacob in the Old Testament? He fell in love with Rachel. He was so smitten with her that he told her father, in Genesis 29:18, "I'll work for you seven years in return for your younger daughter Rachel." This man was willing to work not seven months but seven years for the privilege of marrying this woman. He saw her as a woman of great value. In verse 20, it says, "So Jacob served seven years to get Rachel, but they seemed like only a few days to him because of his love for her."

Has someone told you that your standards are too high? You think too much of yourself? They may be too low. Jacob gladly worked seven years for Rachel's hand in marriage. The story doesn't end there. Jacob's father-in-law tricked him, and he had to work fourteen years to have the right to marry Rachel. There is no record of his complaining about working those extra seven years.

When I encourage you to control *you*, don't judge, mind your own business, be likable, and be confident in your value, I'm not talking about having an attitude of arrogance or pride. Instead, it's a God-confidence rooted in the knowledge of who you are: a daughter of the King. Years ago I met a woman who impressed me with how she carried herself. She lived in London and was visiting Washington, DC. The more I talked with her, the more I sensed a regalness about her. She was self-assured as a Christ follower, but there was something more. It came out in the conversation. She told me that in her native country, Nigeria, she came from a royal line. I said to her, "I could tell there was something different about you. Your posture, your poise, your confidence." She responded: "Oh, yes, from the time I was born, I was taught how I should conduct myself as a member of royalty." In her presence I found myself correcting my posture.

She was taught her value and the protocol of those with royal blood. You are part of the most prestigious royal family. Our Father is committed to teaching us how to carry ourselves so we always reflect our lineage. We should always set the standard in any environment. If you learn to control and value *you*, it will transform your life and lead to your God-given distinction.

216

becoming distinctly you

1. Who or what have you been guilty of attempting to control? Did it work?

2. What is important to remember if you engage in the habit of judging others?

3. "Mind your own business." On a scale of 1 to 10, how often do you get involved in the affairs of others? What boundaries do you need to set to end this practice?

4. What can you do to become more likable?

5. Are you confident in your value?

6. How should knowing your worth impact how you carry yourself and what you choose to control?

—— *Nugget* ——

Develop an action plan for becoming more likable. Ask the Lord to show you *you,* and what needs enhancing in the likability department.

Notes

Part One: Distinctly You Blockers

6: Fickle Feelings

1. A. R. Bernard, Twitter post, February 4, 2015, 5:01 a.m., https://twitter.com/ARBernard.

2. Ravi Zacharias, "A Life That Lost Its Focus: Saul," Ravi Zacharias International Ministries, December 29, 2012, http://rzim.org/let-my-people-think-broadcasts/a-life-that-lost-its-focus-paul-part-1-of-2.

3. Hannah Whitall Smith, in Mary Wilder Tileston, *Daily Strength for Daily Needs* (New Kensington, PA: Whitaker House, 1997), reading for August 24.

7: Distractions

1. Oswald Chambers, *My Utmost for His Highest* (Grand Rapids, MI: Discovery House, 2012, rev. ed.), reading for February 11.

2. Jean N. Grou, in Tileston, *Daily Strength for Daily Needs*, January 12.

11: Spiritual Apathy

1. Charles R. Swindoll, "Erosion," *The Pastor's Blog*, February 18, 2014, http://pastors.iflblog.com/2014/02/erosion-2.

12: Seeing Failure as Final

1. Gillian Zoe Segal, *Getting There* (New York: Abrams, 2015), 19.

Part Two: Distinctly You Builders

14: Do Your Best

1. Jean N. Grou, in Tileston, *Daily Strength for Daily Needs*, January 24.

17: Limit Limitations

1. Fanny J. Crosby, *Fanny J. Crosby: An Autobiography* (Peabody, MA: Hendrickson, 2008), 24.
2. "Joyce Meyer Leads Her Father to Faith," *Charisma Magazine*, April 30, 2002, www.charismamag.com/site-archives/134-peopleevents/people-events/613-joyce-meyer-leads-her-father-to-faith.

19: Soul Fitness

1. "My Hope Is Built on Nothing Less," Edward Mote, 1797–1874.

20: Designer Wardrobe

1. Matt T. Friedman, "Is Meekness Weakness?" *Discipleship Journal* 45 (1988): 19.

Acknowledgments

Many thanks to:

My dear friend Bev Cotton, who believed in this project from the very beginning, dreamed of its impact, and urged me to write the book. You are a great encourager and distinctive graphic designer.

My long-time sister-friends who are always there for me, know the *real* me, and love me anyway: Pat Lawson Muse, Doris McMillon Miller, Audrey Easaw, Paulette Ricks, and Jennifer Robinson—so glad you are in my life. I rejoice in knowing that you are always praying for me. God knew I needed each of you for my journey.

Rhonda Walker, my cousin (who's like a sister), I love and admire you so much! I appreciate your kind and gracious spirit and your modeling what a great wife looks like. Only *we* know what we've been through.

Pastor John K. Jenkins and his bride, Trina, thanks for believing in me and the ministry of *Excellent Living*. Your encouragement speaks volumes. I have watched you closely and learned by your example of humility and generosity.

My career mentors: Burt Perrault, Dave Oseland, and Susan Robinson King. God placed you in my life to help bring out the best in me. So glad you chose me to be on your team. And to Robert L. Johnson for giving me wonderful opportunities to thrive at BET.

Deborah Smith Pegues for prodding me to stay the course. You're a bestselling author, but you were never too busy to take my calls or respond to my emails during this process.

Leslie Vernick—our conversation over lunch was a divine appointment. Much gratitude to you for introducing me to your literary agency. God's perfect timing.

My agent, Mary Keeley, who was enthusiastic about this project from the beginning. God knew I needed someone just like you: direct, driven, tough, and tender. Please don't change.

Bethany House for championing this book and seeing its potential. It's been a privilege to work with Andy McGuire and Ellen Chalifoux, who were excited about the project from day one and ensured it became a better book. To the rest of the publishing team, much gratitude for your input.

My heavenly Father . . . my heart is full of gratitude that you knew me before I was born and knew that a little girl growing up in the inner city desperately needed your hand to guide her through all the vicissitudes of life and to make her feel special. Thanks for choosing me. My best decision ever was to accept you, as a child, as my Lord and Savior. May I always be fully committed to you.

About the Author

Whether it's on television, radio, before audiences, or one-on-one, **Cheryl Martin** is passionate about being an effective communicator and encouraging women to live with purpose and distinction.

She enjoyed a long-time career in broadcast journalism based in Washington, DC, with stints at the NBC-owned and ABC-affiliate television stations. She was a popular news anchor/moderator during her nearly ten-year tenure at national cable network Black Entertainment Television (BET). Cheryl hosted the network's signature Sunday news analysis program, *Lead Story*. She has interviewed such newsmakers as President Bill Clinton, General Colin Powell, Vice President Al Gore, Secretary of State Condoleezza Rice, and Dr. Ben Carson.

Cheryl now devotes her time to speaking, writing, hosting the weekly radio broadcast *Excellent Living*, and freelance media opportunities. She is also the author of *1st Class Single*.

She received a bachelor's degree in speech (radio-TV) and a master's degree in journalism (broadcast) from Northwestern University.

Cheryl has served on the boards of World Vision US, the Evangelical Council for Financial Accountability, and Wycliffe USA.

To contact Cheryl regarding speaking at your event, ordering resources, or feedback on *Distinctly You*, visit cherylmartin.org.